TO THE
LAST
BREATH

A Memoir of Going to Extremes

FRANCIS SLAKEY

Simon & Schuster

New York   London   Toronto   Sydney   New Delhi

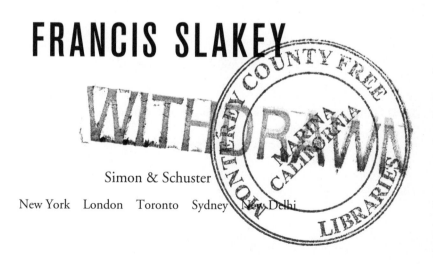

Simon & Schuster
1230 Avenue of the Americas
New York, NY 10020

Grateful acknowledgment is made for permission to reprint articles from the following publications:

"New 'green' pyre to cool planet while burning India's dead" by Tripti Lahiri, Agence France-Presse

"U.S. Links Indonesian Troops to Deaths of 2 Americans" by Raymond Bonner, *The New York Times*

"Indonesia Military Allegedly Talked of Targeting Mine" by Ellen Nakashima and Alan Sipress, *The Washington Post*

Certain names and identifying characteristics have been changed.

First Simon & Schuster hardcover edition May 2012

SIMON & SCHUSTER and colophon are registered trademarks of Simon & Schuster, Inc.

For information about special discounts for bulk purchases, please contact Simon & Schuster Special Sales at 1-866-506-1949 or business@simonandschuster.com.

The Simon & Schuster Speakers Bureau can bring authors to your live event. For more information or to book an event, contact the Simon & Schuster Speakers Bureau at 1-866-248-3049 or visit our website at www.simonspeakers.com.

Designed by Joy O'Meara
Maps by Paul Pugliese

Manufactured in the United States of America

10 9 8 7 6 5 4 3 2 1

Library of Congress Cataloging-in-Publication Data
Slakey, Francis.
    To the last breath / Francis Slakey.
        p. cm.
1. Slakey, Francis.   2. Mountaineers—United States—Biography.   I. Title.
    GV199.92.S59A3 2012
    796.522092—dc23   2011025391

ISBN 978-1-4391-9895-7
ISBN 978-1-4391-9897-1 (ebook)

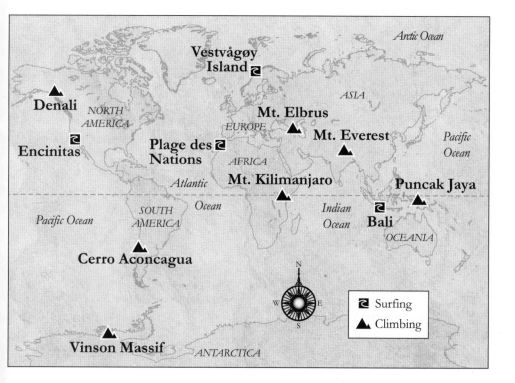

Arctic Ocean

Vestvågøy Island ◙

ASIA

Denali ▲   NORTH
          AMERICA

EUROPE   **Mt. Elbrus** ▲   **Mt. Everest**   Pacific
                                              Ocean

Encinitas ◙

Plage des ◙   AFRICA
Nations

Atlantic   **Mt. Kilimanjaro** ▲

Ocean   Indian   **Puncak Jaya** ▲

Pacific Ocean   SOUTH   Ocean   **Bali** ◙
                AMERICA

OCEANIA

Cerro Aconcagua ▲

N
W   E
S

◙ Surfing
▲ Climbing

Vinson Massif ▲   ANTARCTICA

CONTENTS

CONTENTS

CAST OF CHARACTERS*

In Order of Appearance

Tom Paxton	Climbing partner
Estomii Molell	Masai elder, Tanzania
Most Holy Rinpoche of the Khumbu	Thyangboche monastery, Nepal
Gina Eppolito	Trekker on Mt. Everest, Nepal
Jim Williams	Climbing partner
Ang Nima	Sherpa, Khumbu Valley, Nepal
Mike McCabe	Climbing partner
Patsy Spier	Survivor of the ambush in Papua, Indonesia
Antonius Wamang	Leader of the ambush in Papua, Indonesia
Hassan	Driver, Essaouira, Morocco
Pemba	Drooling mutt
the Fixer	Professional grifter, Lhasa, Tibet
the Snake Goddess	Deity, Bhutan
Kinle	The Lama of Dhorika, Bhutan
Mr. Jayasinghe	Innkeeper, Haputale, Sri Lanka
Agarwal the Engineer	Inventor, New Delhi, India
Knute	Owner, bunkhouse, Vestvågøy Island, Norway

Pictures at: www.ToTheLastBreath.com

---

* The names of some of the people appearing in this book have been changed.

For one who never got the chance and one who, tragically, did

None of us knows what the next change is going to be, what unexpected opportunity is just around the corner, waiting a few months or a few years to change all the tenor of our lives.

—*Kathleen Norris*

TO THE
LAST
BREATH

Chapter 1

BEYOND THE SKY

I am out of balance. I hang dangerously off center but I'm oblivious, until some dim awareness of the world shakes me awake.

I lift my head up slightly and look toward my feet. Sure enough, I'm not flat. My body is sloping downward and I can barely see the tips of my toes in the faint moonlight. This wouldn't be anything to worry about if it weren't for the fact that I'm on a cot pinned to a sheer granite wall two thousand feet above the valley floor.

My shifting around was enough to wake my climbing partner, Tom Paxton. Pax is lean, but with a muscled frame that looks like he could haul a bull if the circumstances called for it. I don't know much about his past, and he knows nothing about mine, and that makes for an ideal pairing. We both live without rearview mirrors, driving ahead through our days, and only when absolutely necessary tapping the brake. Pax never boasts, another admirable quality. There are plenty of climbers who talk and never summit; Pax summits, without complaint or glory.

At the moment, like me, he's trying to make sense of what's

happened to the cot. Since it is just barely long enough and wide enough for the two of us he was bound to sense my slightest motion. We're sleeping head to toe so when he lifts up, he sees that he's sloping dangerously upward—his head is a good ten inches lower than his feet.

We had spent a half hour pinning the cot into the wall to make sure it was secure. We jammed thick aluminum blocks into a crack in the granite face, pulling them tight, wedging them deep into the rock. The blocks are solid, they could hold the weight of an elephant; there's no way that they're coming loose. Something else must be going wrong.

As my eyes adjust to the dark, the strips of webbing that hold the cot together come into focus. The strip attached to one of the corners looks like it is lengthening, stretching out like a rubber band.

After a few moments, I shake off my sleep haze and my brain starts processing things more carefully. I realize that the webbing isn't stretching; our situation is much worse than that. The webbing is unraveling. In a few more seconds the webbing will come completely undone and our cot will drop out from under us. There is nothing we can do to stop that from happening.

"Slake."

"Yeah, Pax."

"We're going to fall."

I look over the edge of the cot, down into the void, and wait for the inevitable.

There was a time when people thought that El Capitan could not be climbed. It is easy to understand why. The hammerhead of granite bursts out of the ground and rises straight up, three thousand sheer vertical feet, looming over Yosemite Valley in central California.

Nothing man has ever built has stood this high. Even after a century of hoisting scaffolding, welding steel, and pouring concrete, no building on the planet reaches even two thirds the height of El Cap. When you stand at its base, arch back, and look up, it seems to rise without end, farther than the limits of vision, past the bounds of Earth, pushing up and beyond the sky.

Magnificent, imposing, the rock taunts you, daring you to climb it. There was no question that one day someone would try.

Early attempts were unsuccessful for a simple reason: humans aren't built to scale a smooth vertical wall. We don't have sticky pads on our feet, like a gecko. We don't have the clinging legs of a centipede or the hooves of a mountain goat. Flat and long, our feet are best designed to propel us off flat ground, away from an oncoming mastodon.

To scale a crack in a vertical wall, your legs and feet have to be used in ways that aren't part of our evolutionary development: you pivot a knee out wide to one side, slide your toes into the crack in the rock face, and then twist and press down on the foot with all your body weight, mashing your toes hard into the crack and locking your foot into place. The bones of the foot are compressed and twisted, crushed to conform to the profile of the crack.

The hands follow the same pattern: fingers, knuckles, a fist all getting mashed and pivoted into the crack. The granite is unforgiving and the hand placements need to be precise. If a hand slides against the rough granite, the rock flays off a layer of skin like a potato peeler.

Twist, crush, repeat—that is the methodical technique that propels a climber up the crack in a vertical rock face.

If at some point the crack thins out, too narrow to mash in a foot, then the climber searches for options, balancing on features and contours often no thicker than a nickel, or smearing the rubber of the climbing shoe on the rock, hoping that friction alone is sufficient to stay pinned in place.

If all else fails, climbers come back down and look for a new route.

But now they face another evolutionary disadvantage. Our eyes are well placed when we're climbing up since we can have good visibility of our foot and hand placements. In down climbing, the view is obscured, the balance less assured, the toe sweeps the air searching for the placement.

So the granite monolith of El Cap was unyielding and the requirements for scaling it were inhuman. The climber who would be the first to conquer it would have steady nerves, astounding patience, and a body fully adapted to scaling the vertical world.

Warren Harding, the climber who first scaled El Cap, was an inspiration to me. I was fourteen years old when I first heard about his climb. From that moment on, I wanted his adventure to be my adventure.

His adventure began in the summer of 1957 when he and his two teammates dropped their gear at the base of El Cap like so many other climbers had before them. They carefully pieced together their route, zigzagging up yard by yard. They established camps in the sheer rock wall. They linked their camps with ropes fixed into the rock with pitons—hammering the four-inch-long metal spikes into the cracks—then returned back down to the valley floor.

Progress was slow; too slow. After four laborious months, with the cold settling in and snowstorms approaching, the team was forced to halt the climb for the winter. El Cap was crushing them.

The next summer there was more disappointment. One of Harding's teammates fractured a leg; the other was discouraged and dropped out. It seemed that El Cap would defy another attempt. Harding, determined and fixed on the prize, found two new climbing partners and faced the stone once again.

Months ticked by as the team continued to push upward, establishing a few dozen more feet of the route each day and then descending back down to the valley floor to rest. As fall approached, the fixed ropes began fraying. Weakened and unraveling after a year of use, the ropes would never last through another winter. If the team couldn't scale El Cap before the snows came, nearly eighteen months of work would be lost. It was now or never for Harding.

They loaded up their gear and took to the wall for one final try. With the weather turning and ropes weakening, they knew the odds were completely against them.

The team moved quickly at the start of the climb. It was familiar; they had scaled it dozens of times in going up and down the wall establishing the route. Then hope faded; an early winter storm settled into the valley and they were forced to take shelter on a ledge and wait it out. Days went by; cold rain pounded at the rock, the wind whipped at their backs.

When the storm finally broke, their rhythm was shattered, their morale draining away. Their pace slowed to just five feet an hour—a caterpillar could move faster. They faced a choice: push past the fatigue and go higher; or descend, pack up, forget about El Cap, and get on with their lives.

They decided to push on.

On November 12, 1958, nearly *five hundred days* after Harding started the climb, he and his team hauled themselves over the lip of El Cap. They had done what no one had ever done before, what some people had considered utterly impossible: they had scaled three thousand feet of sheer vertical granite. They had started on a flat valley floor and propelled themselves directly up, straighter than a rocket, directly into the sky.

They challenged nature and suffered a beating for it. Their hands were bloodied and calloused, bodies scarred, feet crushed and bruised. But the day was theirs. They waged war against gravity and, against all odds, had won. They, and they alone, had conquered that colossal piece of granite. As a boy, when I first heard this story, I couldn't imagine a more spectacular ending.

When their feet finally touched the stable ground of the valley floor, there was no press corps to greet them, no microphones or cameras. The public didn't care. Harding's achievement was in the shadow of another, more famous, climb. There was euphoria when Edmund Hillary and Tenzing Norgay summited Mount Everest a few years earlier—their achievement made world headlines. But the conquering of El Cap was a climbing footnote. Harding didn't grumble; instead, he developed a following.

With Harding demonstrating that gravity could be defied, climbers began migrating to Yosemite Valley. They brought with them a new attitude: they swore off the use of pitons. Pounding the metal spikes into the wall severely damaged the rock, disfiguring it, leaving streaks of rust and widening the cracks. And since many of the pitons were left behind in the rock, climbers began viewing it as a garbage trail.

Climbers developed alternative hardware that would allow an ascent without leaving a trace. The piton was replaced with machined bits of metal and camming devices that a climber could slip into fissures of the rock, and the second climber, following behind, could pull out on ascent.

Over the decades, gear became lighter, sturdier, allowing for cleaner ascents that didn't scar the rock. With the new gear came speed; Harding's five-hundred-day ascent was cut down to seven days, then three, then two. Pitons were replaced by equipment with names like bat hooks, Camelots, Ball Nutz, and Big Bros. The new equipment made Harding's gear look like museum pieces: quaint and unreliable.

On our climb of El Cap, Pax and I have all that modern gear with us and we're confident that every piece is 100 percent reliable, manufacturer-tested and -approved. I have been climbing for years and I have never known the gear to fail—mine or anyone else's. Never. The likelihood of a critical piece of equipment actually breaking is vanishingly small, say, one in a million.

I look back now and realize that suffering the astronomically unlikely one-in-a-million event should have given me a sense of foreboding. Instead, that improbability would govern my next ten years, challenging a sense of imperviousness that I had proudly cultivated. At the moment, those unlikely odds are governing the next tenth of a second of my life.

Thwwwwip. The last few stitches of webbing unravel and the cot drops out from under us.

Before we had gone to sleep we were careful to tighten our harnesses around our waists and clip them onto ropes secured onto the rock face. But the ropes have some slack, so as the cot drops out beneath us, we begin to fall until the rope goes taut, takes our weight, pivots our feet under us, and then pulls us toward the wall, slamming us into the rock.

We hang there in the darkness, our only protection a strand of nine-millimeter-thick rope that keeps us from plunging two thousand feet to the valley floor.

If either of us had tied a meager knot or were loosely clipped into the anchor, we would be in free fall right now, moments away from having the life crushed out of us. In the history of El Cap climbing, dozens of climbers have met that fate. But having avoided that ourselves, there is comfort now, ease. It is a remarkably peaceful moment.

I walk my feet up the rock face a few steps and lean back on the rope, staring up at the night sky.

Breathe in, breathe out. Calm.

With the immediate danger past us, we now have to focus on the next dilemma. We are dangling like puppets in the pitch black of night. We need to find a way out of this.

I have no idea how much of our gear plunged to the valley floor below. That will become all too clear the next day. For now, what we need most is some light.

A fifteen-foot circle of light cuts through the darkness, spotlighting the granite. The beam of Pax's headlamp starts to move across the rock wall, slowly rastering back and forth.

I unclip my headlamp from a belt loop on my harness and join the search, sweeping my light across the sheer granite face, scanning for a place—a ledge, a cave, a protrusion—anywhere to take the weight off our harnesses and rest.

Pax finds it first. "There's a ledge," he calls out. Those are the first words spoken since the cot collapsed and if he'd yelled that out at midnight at one of the populated camps in the valley below, he would have awakened someone who would yell at us to shut up. But here, thousands of feet above them all, we're out of earshot and his words are welcome news.

Pax's headlamp is illuminating a feature in the rock that is roughly twenty feet below us and ten feet off to the side. It's a small ledge, smaller than our collapsed cot, only about the size of a couple two-by-four planks. It is meager, just a fraction of scaffolding, but it is the only option we have.

"Looks comfortable, Pax. Let's get down there." With that, I shift my headlamp's beam back to my harness. We have to untie from the safety rope we've been dangling on and clip onto another rope—one long enough to reach the ledge below.

From my harness I unclip a rappel device, a thick, sturdy figure 8–shaped piece of metal that fills the palm of my left hand. With my right hand I thread a rope through the top loop of the 8 and then clip the bottom loop onto the harness. I take in the slack and lean back on the rope. It takes my weight.

The only thing in my vision now is the rope tied onto my harness;

the rest of the world once again falls back into darkness. It's time to untie the safety knot.

This is a moment that might give some people pause. The safety line is secure: it rescued us from a two-thousand-foot plunge; it has proven its reliability. The rappel line, on the other hand, hangs loosely below my feet, untethered and swaying in a modest breeze. One could imagine a cascade of problems that might result in shifting to that untested line.

That is certainly one way to size up the options: untested versus proven. But that would be the wrong way to look at it. If I assessed things that way, I would never have gotten off the ground to do this climb in the first place.

Here's the way I see it: either I untie the safety line and rappel through the open air down toward the ledge; or I continue to dangle on the safety line with no possibility of rest or relief. It's not a complicated situation. I untie the knot without hesitation.

Lowering is easy, but that won't get me to the ledge. If all I do is rappel straight down I'll pass by the ledge, which is ten feet off to my right side. So as I lower down, I'm looking for a way to climb over to the ledge. But nothing appears. In the glow of my headlamp all I see is smooth, featureless stone; there aren't any cracks or holds that I can use to haul myself over.

There are features to my left, and that will have to do. I'll climb up and over to my left, and then I'll have to let go of the rock and try to swing over to the ledge.

I lower down until the ledge is just about at eye level and then I start climbing up to my left. When I think I'm at the necessary height, I pause for a breath, then I lean back on the rope, pull my feet in, and let go.

I swing free, into the darkness, penduluming to the right.

I rise up and over the ledge and drop my feet down on the flat, firm surface. Done. I'll get some rest tonight. I can relax now, reflect.

The superstar of El Cap, Warren Harding, no doubt faced a moment like this. To succeed, he had to shrug off crises without concern. His team members had dropped out, his equipment was nearing failure, the weather was unforgiving, the summit desperately out of reach. What kept Harding climbing?

I think the answer is this: Harding's spine was fortified with steel, and it gave him a cool indifference to disaster.

That evening on El Cap, with my back leaning against the cold granite and my feet hanging over the rock ledge, I thought about what just happened. My nerves had been steady; I was calm and detached. I hadn't always been this way. Growing up, I hadn't been the kid who at two years old was fearlessly scaling bookcases or balancing on slender tree branches. I had become this way.

When I was eleven years old my Ecuadorian mother, Zaida Sojos-Vela, died from brain cancer. The struggle ended, and death was accepted, on the day when the doctor matter-of-factly explained to my father that they had just tried the last drug that was available.

"There is nothing left to do. Zaida will die within a couple months."

My father described that moment to me when I was a few years older, old enough to understand the direness of the event. In his telling me the story his voice had acquired the very same clinical dispassion of the doctor, though I'm sure that when he heard the words, rather than when he told me the words years later, he was devastated.

I had been preparing for that moment, my mother's death, for years. I saw her long slow grinding decline, from cane, to walker, to wheelchair. Then, near the end, I wouldn't see her for days at a time as she suffered quietly, lying flat, behind the closed door of her bedroom.

That last time she came out of the bedroom was to do something for me, to cut some brownies out of the tin that my father had made for my birthday. She was laying on the sofa in the living room, my father at her side, when I walked into the kitchen and saw the unevenly cut jagged pile of brownies. I assumed it was my dad who had blundered around with the knife.

"Who cut these? They're all messed up."

Those were the last words my mother heard me speak. A week later my father ushered me and my brothers in to her hospital bedroom for one last visit. Her mind was drifting by then, lubricated by morphine. She had no idea who I was. It was then that I recognized the impact of what I had said a few days earlier.

I'm sure she felt dismay at not being able to do something so modest as slice me a few brownies on my birthday. It probably took what little energy she had left in her just to lift the knife. My ungrateful, foolish words cut far more deeply.

There was nothing I could do to correct those final words I'd said to her. As I saw it, at eleven years old, I could either be weighed down by regret or act like it never happened. I chose the latter path.

Days later, my mother was buried. I remember returning home from her funeral and playing table hockey with a friend. I forced our typical banter as the puck bounced around the metal frame. With my eyes dry, I worked desperately to treat the day like it was any other. That sounds heartless as I confess it now. Yet, after witnessing her years of slow painful deterioration and telling her those final words, I reacted by thickening my defenses. I decided that I would never again let something cut into me so deeply. For decades I allowed my life to drift along with little warmth or purpose. As I grew older, I kept mostly to myself, lived by my own rules, and stayed on the move.

The next morning Pax and I assess our situation. The cot, dangling flat against the rock wall above us, is ruined; we won't be using it again. With no place to sleep between here and the top of the wall, we have no choice now. We must finish the climb before nightfall. To do that, we need to lighten our load.

Pax grips the cot, arms spread wide, a corner in each hand, and looks over at me. We are 2,500 feet straight up and there isn't a soul below us. While Pax holds the frame, I unclip it from the hauling rope.

"Adios," Pax says. He lets the cot slip out of his hands.

This can work out just fine, I remember thinking as we watch the cot plummet straight down, picking up speed. Sure, it will be mangled when it hits bottom, but we can collect all the parts, box them up, and send them back to the manufacturer with an explanation of what happened. Maybe they'll replace it, no money lost. And the money was key. We were living on a lean budget, and buying a new $800 cot wasn't a possibility.

As the cot continues its free fall, it catches some wind. It pauses its downward plunge as the end turns flat and it transitions from a straight-down fall into a graceful arch.

"That sucks," Pax sums up our situation. "Keep your eye on it," he yells, eyes squinting in the sun, hand flat over his eyebrows. "We have to get that cot back when we get back down."

As the cot starts to drift away from the wall of El Cap, for the first time in all the times I've climbed here, I actually look out over the valley. I had always been so consumed by the climb that all I ever saw was the block of granite in front of me. I would only see the cracks, the lines, the paths upward.

Now, for the first time, I'm actually getting a sense of the place. I've turned my back to the granite and am seeing Yosemite for the first time.

The cot is flitting in the wind now, riding the current, butterflying on the gusts. It no longer seems like pieces of hard aluminum fastened together with bolts. It is gliding like a bird slipping across the horizon, down over the colossal unclimbable redwoods—straight as flagpoles and hundreds of feet tall—that fill the valley floor.

On any typical day, dozens of spectators look up at El Cap with binoculars and telescopes keeping watch on climbers. They are there now, watching all this unfold.

"You know," I realize, looking down at them dotting the valley floor, "there's no way they can figure out why we just did that." It would be like watching a neighbor toss his bed out a window.

I'm hoping that one of the spectators will now do the neighborly thing. So long as the cot continues its path out into the valley, it will clear the redwoods and drop down into the clearing. Perhaps one of the observers will collect the cot and hold on to it for us.

Then the wind shifts slightly and the cot changes its glide pattern. It begins to make its way back to the base of El Cap, away from the clearing. This could be even better. If it lands at the base of the climb, we can pick it up on our way out. Our luck, I thought, just might be improving.

Suddenly, the cot stops moving. It comes to rest on top of a two-hundred-foot-tall redwood tree.

Over the next several hours we cover the last five hundred vertical feet to the top of El Cap. Our pace is steady, deliberate. We adhere to the mantra of climbing: economy of motion. Preserving the necessary energy requires that a climber make no unnecessary moves, that positions are optimized with the arms providing balance, the legs the propulsion. Bulk is a liability; a clear mind an asset. Goliaths don't rule the rock, Davids do.

As climbing evolved from the lumbering five-hundred-day ascent by Harding to quicker harder climbs, the sport required better fitness, higher strength-to-weight ratio, more poise, and greater flexibility. Climbers became athletes. But they didn't have the muscled physique of a football running back. Instead, leaner was better and women were as competitive as men. In fact, a woman holds one of the most coveted records in the history of Yosemite climbing. In 1993 Lynn Hill became the first person to ascend El Cap—the very same route as Harding—without using a single piece of equipment to haul herself up. As remarkable as that was, a year later she repeated that feat with blazing speed, this time going from the valley floor to the top in less than twenty-four hours.

Pax and I continue up the rock face. I move at a snail's pace compared to other climbers. Yosemite draws the best climbers in the world, and there is always someone better than me, often right on my tail. This route Pax and I are on will take us two and a half days. Three weeks from now, a team from Germany will do this route and set a new speed record: seventeen hours.

That accomplishment will be overshadowed by the feat of another climber, a member of a unique breed of human: the free soloist.

Buffeted by supreme confidence, the free soloist scales the rock without ropes or a partner. And here the tales of Yosemite reach mythic scale.

There is the story of the free solo climber who reached a section of rock, 2,500 feet up, that had a crack too small for him to plug his fingers into. So he pulled out two small pieces of gear, put one in each hand, then alternately reached up and plunged them into the quarter-inch-wide crack and hauled himself up with a series of one-armed pull-ups. One missed gear placement and he would fall a half mile straight down to his death. He made it without incident, without even sweating, so the story goes.

I know that some people believe that free soloists are foolhardy.

But I can think of only one word to describe what these people do: necessary. This is the only way they would think of climbing. And they have to climb.

Like most climbers, I dabbled in free soloing. Once, when I was alone, scaling a block of granite and about forty feet off the ground, I lost my balance. My right foot was on a thin ledge, my left foot, unsupported, hung free off to the side, providing a counterweight. A few fingers on my left hand were braced against a quarter-inch-deep vertical notch, allowing me to lean my body to the right.

I couldn't hold this position for long, but I wouldn't need to. I moved my body further to the right and reached several inches above me to what seemed like a reliable handhold. I had thought the hold was a solid pocket, deep enough to slip up to the first knuckle of two fingers. As my fingers neared the feature, I realized that it was merely a discoloration—there was no pocket.

This is when a climber pauses and reevaluates, pulls back and analyzes, searches for a new route. I had been able to carry out precisely that type of rational detachment in countless situations before. Not this time.

As I review that moment now, the only reason I can offer for not making that cool detached climbing assessment is that I thought I had done all the planning I needed to when I was on the ground sizing up the route. I was now executing my very deliberate plan. When I reached up for that pocket I had already determined that it was the only way up. There was no other route; I was committed. There was no way to down climb.

I made a mental shift. When what I thought was a pocket turned out to be nothing more than smooth rock, I accepted that I was going to hit the ground. Instead of evaluating options for going up, I began to prepare myself for the fall.

At forty feet high on an eighty-five-degree-angled slab of rock, I could manage the fall if I could roll when I hit, displacing the energy in the impact. The alternative would be a disaster. If I hit the ground flat-footed and rigid, the impact would go straight up my back and cause a compression fracture in my spine.

I looked down at the ground and my right foot popped off the ledge, as if my body simply conceded the inevitable and yielded to gravity.

I don't remember the fall. I covered that distance in little more than a second. What I do remember is hearing a snapping sound when I hit the ground and rolled.

I took stock: there was no blood on the ground, no pain in my arms or back. So far, so good. My right leg was fine; the left leg was throbbing. Staring at my toes, I pivoted the left foot, moving it forward and back. Yes, it hurt, but there was mobility. Perhaps I had imagined that I heard a snap? I stood up. I could put weight on my left leg just enough to walk. I headed back along the leaf-strewn path to the car and drove to the emergency room.

"Does this hurt?" the doctor asked, pressing in on my swollen left ankle.

"Not much." It was painful, sure, but it wasn't a scream-out-loud ache. "Maybe a four on a ten-point pain scale."

"And this?" he kept asking while pressing down in a few more places, twisting the foot.

"Not a problem." Nowhere did the pain seem extreme.

"You did some damage. Clearly. But it's just strained ligaments, not a break."

I liked what I was hearing. This fall would not deter me from climbing. If anything, it would send me back: I had taken a long tumble and came out of it with my limbs intact.

"Ice it for the next couple days. Then switch to a heat pad."

I limped out of the emergency room, confident that I'd be back on rock in a week.

Over the next two days the swelling eased a touch; aspirin moderated the ache. Then, on day three, I switched to a heat pad.

In the first few seconds of applying heat, I felt a comfortable warmth, a friendly hand encircling my muscle and bone. I leaned back on the couch, letting the pad work its heat into my leg.

As the heat stimulated more blood flow, the hand began to squeeze, gripping tight, getting blazing hot. In the fraction of a second it took me to sit up, I experienced the most intense pain of my life. It felt like my leg was about to explode. I peeled off the pad and hurled it across the room.

Waiting in the emergency room for the second time in three days, the magazines were all familiar. So I just stared at the wall until the nurse called my name.

This time, the doctor took an X-ray. This had to be more than ligament damage.

As I sat staring at the walls, waiting for the results, I noticed a group of doctors at the door. One of them pointed at me and then whispered to the others. They saw me staring at them and knew I wanted an explanation. Finally, one of them spoke up.

"Are you Slakey?"

"Yes." I was wondering what could possibly make me a spectacle.

"So, you're the guy who's been walking around on a broken leg for the last three days?"

The X-ray couldn't have been clearer. It was a corkscrew break, twisting up and around my fibula. Evidently, it wasn't my imagination; there really had been a snapping sound when I had hit the ground. And as I twisted and rolled, my left foot hadn't responded fast enough. It stayed in place a bit too long, and my pivoting body had literally twisted the bone, cleaving it into two pieces.

"We should have taken an X-ray the first time. But you said it didn't hurt. Why not?" the doctor asked, genuinely curious.

"A break doesn't hurt as much as you think it would." If I were back there today, I would still rate it a four on a ten-point scale.

"You came back just in time." The doctor explained that the bone was trying to heal itself. To do that, the edges of the two pieces of the fibula had softened into putty. The soft edges were trying to reconnect and harden into place to repair the bone. The problem was that I had interfered with the process by walking around on the leg for three days. As a result, the bone edges would soften, get displaced by my walking, soften some more, get displaced again, and so on.

"In another day," he said, handing me the X-ray slide, "the two pieces of the bone would have slid right past each other. Your leg would have collapsed to half its length." I would have been walking along and the leg would suddenly crumple, like a collapsible telescope.

I would find out years later that the doctor had been overly dramatic that day. My brother, an orthopedic surgeon, explained it to me.

"No, your leg wouldn't crumple, but I know why he said it."

I couldn't imagine why.

"You were walking around on a broken leg. You weren't going to listen to reason. It was the only way he could think of to make you take it seriously."

The doctor's words had their desired effect. I never solo climbed again. To fortify that decision, for years after the fall, I reminded myself of that corkscrew break by using the X-ray as my computer mouse pad.

"That sucks," Pax says for the second time of the climb, his gear strewn out on the ground around him.

We just topped out on El Cap a few minutes ago and I'm lacing up my boots. "What happened?"

"My boots, they're missing."

That's rough news because he needs them for the descent. Climbing shoes have a tight fit, like a ballerina's toe shoes. When you're climbing, the tightness is ideal because it maximizes the sensitivity your toes can have to the rock. But on descent, when you are working your way down steep rocky trails, if you wore those climbing shoes then your feet would take a bloody beating. Instead, you wear boots.

Pax's boots aren't actually missing; we both know exactly where they are. Since they aren't in the pile around his feet, they must be three thousand feet below us, having gone airborne when the cot fell out from under us.

As I look back on that moment I see several ways we could have handled the next six hours. I could have gone down, picked up an extra pair of boots from a friend at camp, and hiked them back up the trail for Pax to use. I didn't do that; I'm embarrassed now to admit that it didn't even occur to me. I could barely even manage to give him much sympathy.

"You're right, that does suck," was all I said.

And so, without complaint, Pax hiked down in his climbing shoes, the sharp rocks on the trail pressing up and through the thin rubber. As expected, the six hours on the trail left his feet beaten and worn. When we got back to the car, he pulled his climbing shoes off and it looked as though his feet had been whipped with a bamboo cane.

That night, back in camp, with Pax's feet airing out in the cool breeze, we considered the next dilemma: the cot was sitting on the top of a two-hundred-foot-tall redwood tree.

"Pax, I'd like to help, pal, but I gotta get back home to work."

"I totally understand."

Again, I look back on that moment, years later, with embarrassment. I didn't offer to help. I didn't even offer to pay for a new cot.

"No problem, Slake, I'll scale the tree and get it myself."

I called Pax a few weeks later to find out what happened. Tom

Paxton had probably become the only climber in the history of Yosemite to ever scale a redwood tree.

The cot was mangled, but he broke it down into parts, stuffed them into a box, and sent them back to the manufacturer with a note explaining what happened, redwood tree and all.

With a boxful of parts, the manufacturer would have no way of knowing whether Pax's story of our climb was true. There was plenty of reason to reject his request for a refund. The likelihood of a cot breaking the way it did is infinitesimally small—one in a million. But they took him at his word.

1 in 1,000,000.

That astronomically small likelihood would govern a journey that would take more than a decade of my life to finish.

The journey would completely unravel me, then bind me back together into someone who could feel and care. I look back now and I don't even recognize the callous nail-driving mallet that I was. By crisscrossing a world of mountains and oceans, I would eventually discover my humanity.

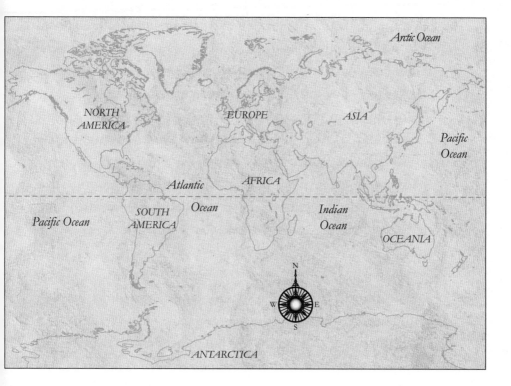

Chapter 2

BE STRONG

My journey began with a simple plan to climb the highest mountain on every continent and surf every ocean. Other climbers had already summited the mountains, someone may even have surfed all the oceans, but no one had done the combination.

I was thirty-seven years old, with no permanent ties. I had taken my career as a physicist in a direction that gave me enough flexibility to travel for weeks at a time. Being a scientist, I would work through the list of mountains and oceans with perfect efficiency, carefully assessing each challenge, evaluating risks, and completing tasks.

I wasn't trying to bring meaning or purpose to my life or anyone else's. I wouldn't add one dime to a charity. No one would be any better for my journey, and that was just fine with me.

I had been living with that indifference to the world, that detachment, for decades. My separation from others began when I was eleven years old, during a short walk down a stark hallway.

I can't remember the last time I was in this room. For months, the door has been shut, sealed tight, a tomb. Occasionally, when I walked down the hall, I stopped at the door to check for any sounds. There was no hushed conversation, not even the soothing tones of a radio. I imagined that if I pressed my eleven-year-old ears hard to the door I might at least be able to hear my mom breathing. I never heard a sound.

The door was open as I walked by this time and I stood in the doorframe and looked in. The bedroom was empty. My father must have taken Mom to the living room; she must be feeling better today.

Across the room I could see two bulges of Styrofoam on the dresser. Draped over the top of one of them was a familiar spread of dark hair. I recognized the trim front, the straight sides, the curl at the bottom. I walked to the dresser, reached over, and tugged the wig off the featureless head.

I couldn't remember ever running my fingers through my mother's hair. Now, I was curious to feel its softness. My fingertips pressed into the strands. The hair was dry and stiff. I flattened the curl in my palm, but it resisted, retreating back to its manufactured shape the moment I let go.

I don't recall if I placed the wig back on the foam, but I remember walking out of the room and then back down the hallway toward the living room.

By then my mother had all she could take of the day; my father was now bringing her back to the bedroom. She was spread across his chest, her back resting gently over his left arm, knees suspended by his right arm, her legs hanging down toward the floor. As we approached each other, my father turned sideways, his back to the wall, my mother's body now just a few inches from my right shoulder.

No glance was exchanged; no words said. We passed in silence.

I'm sure that she ached to reach out and touch my hand. But, true to her character, she wanted no pity; she did not want to provoke tears.

A few moments later, as I continued down the hall, I heard the click of the bedroom door pulling shut behind me.

No words were exchanged when I passed my mother, but I heard her nevertheless. Over the years that followed, I would recall that moment and I could still hear her voice. And even though her head was turned, tucked deep into my father's chest, I could see her eyes as she spoke to me. With the strongest of hearts, and clearest purpose, she told me this: *be strong*.

And so I followed her advice. My skin thickened.

It would take me another thirty years and a journey of tens of thousands of miles, deep into the heart of the world, before I realized that I totally misunderstood my mother that day.

I suppose that there was a chance, a few years after my mother's death, to reverse my growing detachment. I had formed a solid friendship with an adventurous kid my age.

Greg Stevens and I are standing on a mountaintop overlooking a valley near Logan, Utah. I was spending my summer break from high school here and had made friends with Greg. Energetic, lively, full of curiosity, he was immediately likable.

We drove up here, along with a busful of other kids and a couple of parents, and we were now looking out over the mountain, puzzling over whether we could ditch the group and take our own route down.

"Let's climb down."

I was cautious. There was no path down; we would have to find our own way. Sure, things looked straightforward enough from here, but we couldn't see down the entire side of the mountain. It could get dicey.

"If things get hard, then we'll just climb back up," Greg encouraged.

Neither of us were climbers and we didn't have any gear. We could get ourselves into a situation we couldn't get out of.

"I'm not going; let's just take the bus down," I said.

"Well, I'm going. Go ahead and take the bus." Greg walked to the edge and flipped his feet over the rock and started to descend.

I got the news later that afternoon. One of the parents asked around when Greg didn't show up at the bus and found out that he was climbing down the mountain. When he didn't return that afternoon, they contacted the police, who dispatched a helicopter to search the canyon.

Greg had fallen. Unable to move, the helicopter medevaced him to the hospital. The word from the pilots was that he would be okay.

I met Greg's sister in town and we hurried to the hospital. I remember strolling down a hallway and casually asking a passing nurse where a medevaced patient might be: emergency room? waiting room? Maybe Greg was already out of surgery and would be sitting up in his bed, smiling when we walked in the room.

"Who are you looking for?"

"Greg Stevens," his sister answered.

"Oh, he died."

For a moment, there was silence. I remember not understanding the meaning of those three words, the impossibility of them. And then his sister screamed—not in words, just tones, piercing desperate tones that didn't come from the lungs but from the anguish of a crushed heart. Her scream continued on, filling the hallway, sliding under the cracks of doors, pressing against the windowpanes.

I don't recall if I put my arm across her shoulder; if I did, it offered no comfort.

I simply looked ahead, into the nurse's eyes. I could see that she was grappling with the depths of her error. How could she have said those words? Perhaps she was new or inattentive or tired or something that could explain the heartlessness of her response.

I had only one thought at that moment: Greg is gone. Forever.

Two people had been torn out of my life. The lesson I drew then, as a teenager, seemed so obvious, so unmistakably clear: don't form attachments; avoid more loss.

With my growing indifference, it wasn't long before I began running into trouble.

The first snag occurred shortly after I broke my hand in a game of street hockey. It was so badly shattered that the doctor isolated it with pins and wrapped my entire forearm in a cast. "Try to keep it elevated; that will make it heal faster," he advised.

I regarded that advice as an excellent excuse for skipping school, so for the next four weeks I stayed at home without any concern for classes and schedules.

When I did eventually go back to school, I had to confront my tenth-grade history teacher. It wouldn't go well.

I'm standing in front of her, with a test in my left hand, waiting for her rant to end. After months of my battling with her, she is thoroughly enjoying this moment.

She points at the splint on my right hand.

"You were out of school the last four weeks because of that?"

It did look meager. It was just a four-inch-long piece of curled aluminum that rested in my palm and ran up to the tip of my pinkie finger, held firmly in place with a few strips of medical tape. The doctor put that modest brace on after cutting off the cast a day earlier.

"Yesterday I was in a cast that ran from my elbow and closed off my entire hand. I had to keep it elevated, I couldn't write."

She sneered. She disliked me and the feeling was mutual. And she had every reason to doubt me.

Before I broke my hand she and I would have words nearly every class. She routinely ridiculed students. She would pick on just a couple of kids who would quietly suffer under her assaults. It was unfair and I had asked her to back off the harassment and get on with teaching.

As far as she was concerned, this was payback time.

"I've decided to take three points off your grade for every day that you were absent."

My grade just sank to a D.

"Now, let me see that test," she demanded.

I hand her the sheets. This wasn't going well, and I could see where it was heading.

"This test is blank."

"Right," I replied. "I didn't know that there would be a test today and so I wasn't ready to take it. I was hoping to take it in a couple days, after I've caught up."

"You could have studied all those days you were gone. You could have asked a fellow student to bring you the homework so you could keep up."

She was right. "Okay. But can I just take a retest next class? I'll catch up tonight."

"No, you can't. I am giving you a zero on the test."

With that test score and the points she just took off for my absences, there was no way I could recover my grade. No amount of extra credit could revive it, not that she would even consider giving me the opportunity.

I just failed high school history.

The next day, my father took this up with the principal. There were a number of ways the principal could have handled the situation in his siding with the teacher. He could have said that he must allow teachers a certain amount of authority and he was deferring to her. I suppose I could have accepted that. Instead, he explained to my father that I needed to learn a lesson.

Being a teacher himself, my father thought this was the wrong way to teach a lesson—grades weren't effective disciplinary weapons. I was probably overly assertive in class, my father conceded. And yes, I had been impolite and there were certainly better ways of addressing my complaints about the teacher. But there were also better ways to handle this, my father explained.

The principal didn't care. The F would stand, he threatened. And if I persisted in my behavior, which he fully expected would happen, more Fs would follow.

With little possibility of improving my situation at that school, my dad made a decision: he punched the reset button.

I left that school in Virginia and we moved to my grandmother's house in Sacramento. My father thought some grandmotherly hovering would help put some discipline in the life of his youngest teenager. It didn't work. While my father spent nights writing in his study, I would be outdoors, feral, gathering in a pack of friends or strangers to pursue aimless misdemeanors.

Late one night, we break into a gym to play basketball.

When cops arrive, we sprint out the door and scatter. As I'm cutting through yards, I see up ahead a brick wall, low enough to throw my hands over. When I pull up to have a look, I can't believe my luck. Here is something I've been looking for the last two weeks. It's been more than a hundred degrees for days, and I've been looking for a place to cool off. As I drop down off the wall into the apartment complex, there in the patio in front of me and encased in textured, bumpy concrete, is the glimmering water of a swimming pool.

A few days later I'm soaking in the water. The pool is shallower than I thought. I'm standing in the deepest part, my elbows resting on the pool sides, and the water is a few inches below my shoulders. It's also narrower than I thought, about twenty feet wide, and it's squeezed between two four-story apartment buildings. With only about ten feet between the sides of the pool and the buildings, it's shady, but it feels cramped.

The pool is shallow and narrow; there's no diving board and no point in swimming laps since it only takes a few strokes to go from one end to the other. All I can do is wade in the water, brainlessly. I lean my head back wondering how long I can handle being idle, and then, just before I close my eyes, I notice something.

One of the buildings has a fire escape that I could use to get up on the roof. From there, I can walk up to the edge of the building and drop down into the pool. The building can be my diving board.

There's no one here, no one to stop me, so I could go up there right now. But first, a couple things need thinking through. I'd be dropping four stories into less than six feet of water—that seemed a bit tight. I would also need to jump out, not just down, so I could clear the ten feet of concrete from the edge of the building to the pool. I wouldn't want to jump out too far though or else I would pass over the pool and hit the concrete on the other side.

I stare up at the building, puzzling over the odds.

I decide that the pool is a sufficiently big target, even from that height. It has enough width to allow for a reasonable margin for error. I'm confident that with just a bit of push-off, I'll hit water and not the concrete edge.

The depth, on the other hand, troubles me. There is no way I can dive in from that height and survive it. I would plunge in with too much energy, more than the water could dissipate, and my head would split open on the pool bottom.

But what if I jump down feet-first? If I pull my feet up just as I hit the water, then I should be okay.

I could have stayed in the pool and stared up at the building, running numbers in my head, noodling over the different possible outcomes. After all, I came here just to cool off and there was no need to turn it into anything more. I could stay in the water, relax, and pass the time without incident.

Instead, I lift my elbows off the concrete pool edge, turn, push up out of the water, and stroll toward the fire escape, the water dripping off my swim trunks leaving a spotted trail behind me.

The narrow space between the buildings keeps the ladder in the shade, so I can climb it without worrying about scalding my feet. My feet touch the cool metal of the rung and I start pressing my way upward.

When I get up to the roof and walk to the edge and look down I am immediately relieved. As I suspected, the pool appears to be a big target. When I jump, I'll push off a bit, not too hard, and I should hit the water dead center. I have to remember to pull up my feet; that's the real problem here. If I hit straight-legged, my feet would definitely slam hard into the bottom. Would it shatter bones? I hope it won't come to that.

I step up on the building ledge and jump.

My feet hit the water and the splash starts to rise up around me. I pull up my legs, bending into an L, plunging deeper as my back just barely avoids scraping against the side of the pool. My butt slams down hard onto the concrete pool bottom.

I stand up out of the water and put my hands to my head, pulling back my hair. I turn sideways and look at the back of my legs; there's not even a scrape. I'll do it again, but this time I'll make sure I don't cut it so close to the edge.

I jumped a few more times that afternoon, enough to satisfy myself that I could hit dead center. I went back to the pool a few days later, but this time the patio wasn't empty.

"Are you the jackass who jumped off the building?" The tenant was angry and I couldn't understand why. I didn't harm anybody; I didn't destroy anything. I was the only one taking any risk. Why did he care?

"Yeah," I said, staring back at him. "I jumped into the pool. So what? I didn't bother anybody. Nobody was here."

"Well, you ass, kids were watching from the windows. This morning a six-year-old kid climbed up to the roof to jump."

I was stunned; that was never supposed to happen. Before I had a chance to respond, he said the words that ended the conversation.

"Get out of here," he shouted. "Stay away."

I never bothered to ask what had happened to the six-year-old. I turned and walked away thinking that in the future, if I ever took a risk, I would do it with someone like-minded and capable. I would keep everyone else away.

There's one more thing I should admit, for the context of it all. I remember the night that led to my becoming a scientist. I was drunk, foolish, and desperately willing to lie.

I'm a freshman in college and two strangers I met only hours before at a party are using fire extinguishers to spray people below my dorm room window. I had already taken my turn and missed.

Our laughing and our yells out the window are waking up other students on the floor. Deleep, the Indian in the next room over, pushes open my door.

"What are you doing?"

I turn from the window and face him. There's no sensible answer to his question. It's probably one in the morning, and we've had too much to drink.

Not getting a response, Deleep points toward the other two. "Are those guys students?"

I look at their faces. For the first time I realize that they are older, years older, than I am. I'm eighteen, they're probably in their late twenties. They must have crashed the party I just left. Now they are here, all of us acting like vandals. I don't even know their names.

"Yeah? Well try and dodge this!" One of the thugs hoists the fire extinguisher over his head and throws it out the window. The second extinguisher follows a moment later.

I hear screams from below and rush to look out the window. The few people who are out on the street are scattering now, taking a wide perimeter around the dorm. I don't see the extinguishers, but I don't see anybody down on the ground either. Maybe everything is okay.

When I turn back around, Deleep is gone.

"Fellas," I say to the pair, "that guy lives on this floor. He's probably calling the cops right now."

They grab their beers, still laughing, and shout a goodbye over their shoulders. I would never see them again, but in two days' time all of this would begin to determine my future.

I pick up a few beer bottles, walk them down the hall, and drop them in a trash can in the bathroom. I return to my room and brace for what's coming.

The knock on my door comes about fifteen minutes later. The police must have already talked to Deleep, maybe they've even taken information from people who were on the street, because they know most of the story.

"So you were spraying people out that window?"

There are pivotal questions we face in life, and when they come, our answers can determine our trajectory for decades to come. I knew what would happen if I answered that question honestly, with a yes. I would be booted out of college, for good reason. On the other hand, I could deny having anything to do with it.

"Two guys did it. Not me." I said those words as earnestly as I could, and then I just kept on talking. "I didn't know them, I walked out of a party and they followed me, they walked out too, they just started going the same way I did, I didn't tell them to leave, I would have if I knew what they would do, but they didn't leave they just kept walking with me—"

I could have continued going on for minutes without pause, but the cop cut off my stream of blather. "You never saw them before? They just walked into your room?"

It was obvious from his expression that he didn't believe a word I was saying, so his questions continued. Over the next half hour of probing I learned that no one was hurt, fortunately.

"Great, so no damage done?" I said with relief.

"No damage? Somebody could have been killed. Believe me," he was firm, "this broke the law."

As he finished the interrogation, he dropped the big news. "Well, we may have found the other guys already. We also have a witness. We'll know soon if you're telling the truth."

I spent the next forty-eight hours in limbo. I went to classes, but didn't hear a word. I ate, I'm sure, but didn't taste a bite. Then a student on the floor filled me in on developments. That afternoon

Deleep was being called into the police station to look at a lineup of suspects.

I stayed in my dorm room that day, flat on the bed, with the door open, listening for Deleep's arrival. I had a good idea of how this would play out. Deleep would identify the two thugs and they would tell the police that I was involved. Between their testimony and Deleep's eyewitness account, my lie would be exposed. I was just starting my freshman year of college and I was already on my way out.

I heard the key turn in Deleep's door and I spun up off my bed. I wanted to get the news from him, not the police, not the campus administration.

"Deleep. What happened?"

"Well," he said with a smile, "those white people all looked the same to me."

The thugs were never identified; the case was dropped. Given that near calamity, it might be natural to assume that I learned a lesson and that my life quickly improved. But I didn't learn a thing—I had gotten away with it, after all—and so things got worse.

Within five months, I earned a series of Fs and Ds that landed me on academic probation. The probation came on top of the official disciplinary warning the administration levied on me after the fire extinguisher incident. They were sure I was involved, but couldn't prove it, so they issued a stiff warning. I had now exhausted all options. One more incident, no matter how small, one more bad grade, and I would be thrown out.

I would find out years later that my brothers made a bet at the end of my freshman year that I would never graduate, not from this school, not from any school. I admit, they had good reason for the bet. My situation looked grim:

I had no aptitude for languages (I got an F in German).

I couldn't recall key events in world history (a C-).

I lacked focus (I was on academic and disciplinary probation).

I showed no respect for authority (I had several incidents with police).

Regardless of how bad things were, though, I knew that there was something I could always do: I could analyze, dissect, and calculate. Numbers were always more memorable to me than people's names. A formula would penetrate and stick in my mind where faces would fade.

And so, science became my life vest. I would not allow myself to sink, not willingly, not knowing that others were succeeding around me when I was just as capable as they were.

I needed to rapidly elevate my grade point average, start notching A's, so sophomore year I made a practical decision. I became a physics major and bore down.

Over time, my attitude would change. I completely fell for science, for its ability to render cold, detached assessments, predict outcomes, tease order out of the world.

Eventually, after finishing a Ph.D., physics would bring me right back to the place where I nearly went off the rails. I joined the faculty of the very institution from which I was almost booted out as an undergraduate: Georgetown University.

My brother Rog saw it all happen, astounded that I could pull out of my fall, stabilize, and find direction. The summer after my graduation, he gave me a gift.

"Francis," he said shaking his head, still surprised, "this is for you."

I looked down into his hand. "A rock? You're giving me a rock?"

"That's right." He turned his hand over and dropped the rock in my palm. "I want you to remember what you sank like that first year of school. And don't ever forget that you rose above it."

Nearly two decades later, when I walked for the first time into the apartment of the woman who would change my life, I noticed dozens of rocks on shelves, in bowls, across tabletops. She saw me looking at them and explained: "I collect rocks. It reminds me of where I've been. Do you collect rocks?"

"I have one rock," I answered. "It turned out that one was all I needed."

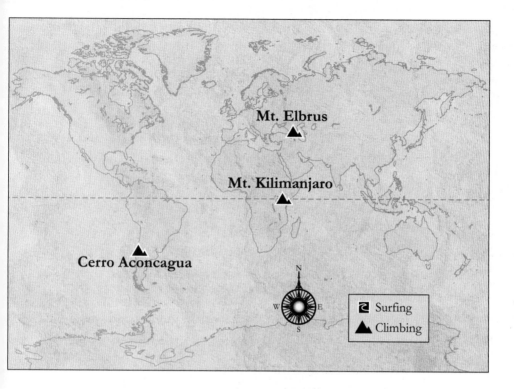

Chapter 3

THREE PILLARS

The moment I decided to set some kind of record may have come on a crisp morning in Wyoming of all places, when my brother uttered one piercing, scarring word to me: "No."

"You can't come with us. It's too dangerous. You're not good enough to climb it."

The only sounds were the snap and clang of carabiners as my two brothers attached climbing equipment to the slings hanging across their chests. The sheer rock wall of Devils Tower rose up behind them, the tip of its granite pillar just starting to catch the glow of the sunrise.

Sure, my brothers were older and more experienced; but I was sixteen and fully capable of managing the risks. I could flash this climb and I had come a thousand miles across the country to prove it.

"You're not going to leave me down here at the base," I demanded. "I came all this way to climb this with you."

"No," is all I remember my oldest brother, Roger, saying. Then they each threw a coil of rope over their shoulder, turned their backs on me, and walked away.

My two brothers would summit that day, and I would watch their slow steady progress up the rock face while sitting under a pine tree, fuming and alone.

That rejection might be the rocket fuel that would propel me to the tops of peaks and across a world of oceans. I would make it clear to them through every mountain and every wave that I was capable— more capable than they would ever be—to manage all the terrain the world could throw at me.

A chip on the shoulder, that's what started it. At least, that's what my brothers think, and they are entitled to their opinion. I would even like it to be true because it might make my motive to climb the highest mountains and surf every ocean seem hard-won and earnest.

My real motive at the time may have been more cowardly and less honorable. The record would conveniently prevent me from forming any deep attachments. It would keep me perpetually in transit, either just getting back from an expedition or just about to leave. I would use my climbing and surfing trips as an excuse when I broke up with girlfriends: "I'm leaving next month for six weeks so I can't have a serious relationship." If I wanted to keep someone at arm's length I would say: "I don't have time for a relationship, I'm training for my next expedition."

The challenge also carried a touch of vanity, the same vanity that made me think I could jump from a rooftop into a pool and survive, or outplay my tenth-grade history teacher. Physics was testing my intellectual limits; this would push me to my physical limits. But for the physical test to be satisfying, it had to be unique. I didn't want to do it if someone else had done it before. I wanted to be first at something.

I look back on it all and those particular motives fade in importance. I understand the journey now; perhaps I didn't at the time. There was really only one purpose for it.

I needed to restore the heart of the boy I had been.

The two aspects of my journey weren't unique. Someone had already climbed the highest mountains. A wealthy entrepreneur named Dick Bass had snatched the record out from under more accomplished climbers for no other reason than he thought of it first.

It was possible that someone had also surfed all the oceans, although there was nothing about it in any record books.

Still, one thing was clear, no one had done the combination. At thirty-seven years old, I would attempt to complete the first global surf-n-turf.

With the skills I had developed through rock climbing—balance, endurance, a solid strength-to-weight ratio, calm under fire—I assumed setting the record would be absolutely straightforward. I would work through the list of mountains and oceans without distraction. Not being independently wealthy, like Bass, the biggest challenge for me, I thought, would be amassing enough money to get to these climbs and oceans. But that seemed manageable. I wasn't married, didn't have kids, and didn't have a mortgage. I could sink every spare dollar I made into the expeditions. If at some point I came up short, I was sure I could find some way to raise the money.

The first step was to start molding my body from a six-foot, 165-pound rock climber into a stouter, thicker 190-pound mountain climber capable of carrying heavy loads under more extreme conditions.

The typical gym fitness measures don't apply when training for mountaineering. It doesn't matter how much you can bench-press, or how fast you can run a mile. Even the percentage of body fat is irrelevant—one of my climbing partners is built like a walrus. Sure, he's heavy, but he compensates for his weight by being utterly impervious to the cold. He can barehand an ice axe in a twenty-five-degree blizzard.

Scientist that I am, I came up with an eggheaded formula that I could use to tell me when I was ready for the mountains:

$$\left(\frac{\text{MAX \# OF PULLUPS}}{\text{RESTING HEART RATE}} \right) \times \left(\text{MAX POUNDS I CAN LEG PRESS} \right) > 400$$

Those numbers all work against each other. If I increase the number of pull-ups I can do, that would lean me out and decrease the amount I can leg-press. If I bulk up to leg-press more, that would increase my resting heart rate. By balancing out all the factors, I determined, I could get an overall high number that indicates I'm prepped for a climb. Of course, my numbers, despite years of training, don't reach Lance Armstrong status. I have a resting heart rate of 39 beats per minute; Armstrong boasts a 34.

I was fit and I had enough funds to get started on the surfing and climbing record. There was one last thing to take care of before starting the journey: I had to take time off from work. The big climbing expeditions, like Everest with its long approach and narrow opportunities for summiting due to weather, would require my being gone at least eight weeks during the spring.

One of my jobs is with the American Physical Society, the professional association of physicists, where I do public affairs work. As it turned out, they were okay with my taking time off; they were even a bit curious as to whether I could pull this off. My other job, as a physics professor at Georgetown University, could have interfered with my plan, but I didn't let it. I had arranged a nontenured position that allowed for minimal commitment; the interests of students didn't concern me at that time. At that point in my life, teaching was mostly about collecting a paycheck.

I had been schooled in teaching science during my years in a graduate program that valued the laboratory over the classroom. As we practiced it, teaching science didn't require engaging with students. The virtue of science is that the answers are factual, derivable, not open to opinion. By contrast, the meaning of a poem is debatable, the value of art is fluid, the impact of a novel is subjective. What differentiates science from all these other pursuits is a clear arrow of progress—each generation builds on the scientific discoveries of the last. All a student has to do is sit back, listen to the lecture, and absorb the mathematical techniques. Conversation isn't necessary.

So I did not ask students how they "felt" about a problem. I didn't need to know their views.

My notes didn't even require updating since most of the problems I taught were solved decades, in some cases centuries, ago.

Here is what a chalkboard would look like after one of my typical lectures:

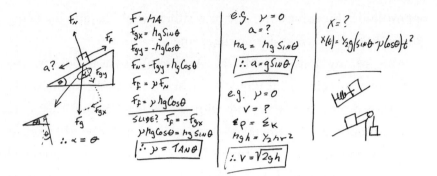

The problem solved on that chalkboard hasn't changed in centuries. Galileo solved it first, four hundred years ago, probably scraping the formulas out in the dirt with his sandal.

What all this meant is that I could turn my back on the students and work at the chalkboard for fifty minutes at a stretch while they diligently scratched out the symbols and methods in their notebooks. Every eight weeks I would pass out a test and ask them to solve variations of the very problems I'd been solving at the board. I could even make the tests multiple choice to keep the time I spent grading to a minimum.

Mechanical, sterile, and with assembly-line efficiency, all students had to do was listen and learn.

Given that impersonal style, there would be no trouble with me scheduling a climb or two each year. I could ask a colleague to fill in on occasion; perhaps I might even assign students some work to do on their own in my absence. I would make sure that my teaching schedule wouldn't hold me back.

My first stop would be Tanzania, in East Africa, to climb Kilimanjaro. As it turned out, the climb went every bit as smoothly as I'd planned, so much so that it was completely uneventful.

The Masai warriors I met, on the other hand, were an entanglement.

———

I crouch down to fit inside the tiny hut made of cow dung and sticks. Once inside, Kilembu offers me a hollowed-out calabash that contains the morning meal: a mixture of cow's blood and milk. Somewhere outside, nearby, are the remains of a village elder who was found dead, dragged out of town, and left for hyenas to devour.

Kilembu picks up his spear, and we crawl back outside. He wears only a red blanket and a pair of sandals that he's fashioned out of a piece of car tire. He introduces me to the key elements of his world, in descending order of importance: two dozen cattle, a few goats, four children, three tiny huts, two wives, a mother. After all the introductions, he takes me back to his cattle for one last look. The cattle are the center of his life. Kilembu lives the typical life of a Masai warrior.

We walk up the hill that rises above the village of Longido. From the top we can see dozens of miles across the African savanna. Kilembu extends his spear out flat to his side, then slowly swings it in front of him.

"All Masai," he says proudly, as his spear traverses the entire length of the horizon.

Yes, as far as the eye can see, this is Masai country. All Kilembu has ever seen is Masai country; he has never stepped a foot beyond it. So far, neither have his children.

Masai are the native tribesmen of Kenya and Tanzania, perhaps as many as a million in number. Despite contact with modern civilization, the vast majority of tribesmen have maintained their centuries-old nomadic life.

Kilembu ends our walk at the home of Estomii Molell, a Masai elder. I duck out of the midday sun and into his dimly lit hut. On the floor, with his arms twisted like corkscrews, lies the paralyzed frame of this village elder. A Masai warrior stands at his side, brushing away flies.

"I want you to know, we are not dirty here," Estomii says. He speaks emphatically, anticipating criticism.

"There is no extra water for washing. When a woman travels fifteen kilometers to get water, and you ask her for some water to wash, what do you think she'll say?"

The point made, his face relaxes. He wants me to understand his people. So he starts by talking about mine.

He says he knows the United States. He knows of its phones and its computers and its big roads.

"Why would we want that?" he asks.

He dismisses all of our modern technological infrastructure with a laugh. "Here we walk and we see people. In the West, you call and you never see."

He explains that our sophisticated telecommunications have left us isolated: "In your country, people have everything but company."

"I went to Germany and stayed with a family," Estomii continues, "and you know the conversation over breakfast? 'Pass the sugar.' And over dinner? 'Pass the salt.'" Estomii chuckles. "I asked this man, 'What is your neighbor doing?' and he said, 'I don't know.'"

Estomii shakes his head in wonder. "In Masai country, you cannot say, 'That is not my business.'" He illustrates his point. "If a boy cringes when he is circumcised, everyone will know the next day. He will never be respected."

Estomii pauses, a chance for a question. I ask about crime.

"Yes, we do have killing here," he says gravely. "A Masai killed a Masai here in 1961. It has happened again this month."

He falls quiet; he is embarrassed by what he thinks is a large number of murders. I'm surprised, because I know what a low number it truly is. In my hometown of Washington, D.C., we were suffering from three murders every week.

"The family of the dead man dragged the body outside the village and left it for the hyenas. Then they demanded the other man pay forty-nine cows. He paid; he is now accepted back."

I'm shocked. "Isn't anyone worried that he might kill again?" I ask.

"No," Estomii says, confused by my question. "That would cost him 189 cows, and he can't afford that."

I'm so stunned by this notion of justice that all I can think to ask is how they determine the number of cows. Estomii says the number varies, but "there must always be a nine"—49, 189, 199. This doesn't clarify anything. I ask, "Why nine?"

He explains: "The nine orifices. A murdered man has been stripped of life from his nine orifices, and that must be repaid."

I stop our conversation to count. When I look back up, Estomii has fallen asleep. His warrior motions for me to leave. As I walk out the door, I notice the warrior's spear leaning against the wall.

Once a week, Masai come from as far as twenty miles away to trade at the makeshift market. Seventy or eighty warriors gather around a pen to trade cattle. No one is buying, few are talking, all look proud. I go look for some shade and stumble across Mwarimbo.

He's built like a Masai—tall, lean, and fit, with an expressive face—but that's where the similarity ends. He is not Masai. He wears pants, a short-sleeved cotton shirt, and sneakers; he asks me to call him "Johnson." He is a teacher at the Longido Secondary School.

"What subject?" I ask.

"Science."

I'm relieved. Finally, I've met someone I can relate to. We start strolling in the direction of his school.

In Tanzania, primary school is free. The primary schools in this part of the country put sixty children into a classroom. The next four years of education make up secondary school—roughly equivalent to our high school—and it must be paid for by the family. The quality of education is much higher, the benefits seem clear, and yet very few

Masai children attend secondary school. It's the father's decision and, for many, education comes at too high a cost.

"At $120 a year, it would mean selling a cow to get a child through secondary school," Johnson explains. But the Masai seem to have plenty of cows to spare, I observe.

Johnson shakes his head. "You don't understand the problem."

The vast majority of Masai men consider education "trouble," he says. "When a girl completes secondary school, she realizes she is more valuable than a cow." That's trouble. Warriors start to define their place in society when they marry and receive a dowry of cattle. They take three wives, get three dowries, start amassing a herd. So educating girls threatens the cattle business; it threatens the Masai way of life. To Masai warriors, education is a raw deal.

We've walked across the savanna for nearly an hour when we reach the cinder block school.

"All they think about is cattle," Johnson continues, barely controlling his anger. He is determined to do whatever it takes to break the Masai of their bond to cattle and to give the children an education.

He explains his method. It is extreme, but as a scientist I appreciate its efficacy.

Johnson's first law: "Masai are not allowed to wear their traditional clothes in this school." Second, they are addressed only by Western names that they are given, not their Masai names. Third, in addition to that initial cultural stripping, Johnson takes a final intense step: all Masai students board at his school. They are not allowed to return home until the school year has finished.

The first thing students learn is that raising cattle, which graze on whatever grows on the savanna, is not a sustainable livelihood. "Agriculture is inevitable," Johnson declares.

Through science courses, students learn basic principles of farming, irrigation, and how to combat drought. They learn about basic medical care and vaccinations; inconceivably, the country is still fighting polio.

But not everything they are taught is so practical. Johnson speaks with zeal about the simple excitement of learning. He wants children to identify with a larger world, a world I have largely ignored.

Before I leave the school, Johnson introduces me to Anna and Susanna. They are Masai, but I never learn their Masai names. They wear skirts and blouses, socks and dress shoes. They speak only a few words of English, but they seem eager to try. We chat for a few minutes. When I say goodbye, they say it was a pleasure to meet me—a verbal curtsy. As they walk away, Johnson explains that they will be leaving the school after only one year here because their father will not pay. According to Johnson, the children want to stay.

The next morning I return to Estomii's hut. I tell him about Johnson, about the school. I ask his opinion of modern education.

"Let me tell you about one of the best brains in Tanzania. Very brilliant with mathematics. He went to Britain to study aircraft design. He came back, and you know what? We don't design airplanes here." Estomii chuckles. "He is still looking for a job."

His warmth has drawn me into the story; we're both laughing as he delivers the clincher: "He is useless."

Estomii adds: "This Johnson is a fool. He is not Masai; he does not understand. Without cattle, Masai have no identity."

Estomii points out that a truly competent teacher would be able to educate children no matter what clothes they wear. "Besides, their clothes are practical. It is hot here, why wear pants?"

As he launches into a bitter criticism of Johnson, I tune out and watch the warrior looking after Estomii brush away flies. Estomii has already made his point. He is engaged in a battle, the only battle that a paralyzed old man with twisted arms and a fading voice can still fight. He fights for his tribe's identity. With a quick mind and a passionate heart, he fights for what it means to be Masai.

I returned to the United States a few days later. Having been gone for several weeks, I knew that I would have mail waiting for me, a pile of bills that needed to be paid. Efficiency dictated that my first stop should be the post office.

"I'm here to pick up the mail I put on hold," I explain to the postal worker. I pull my driver's license out of my wallet.

She glances at the ID and walks into the back and comes back a few minutes later empty-handed. "No mail."

"What? That's not possible. I've been gone for over a month. Of course I have mail. Phone bill, gas bill, credit cards. Did you check the right address?"

"No mail." And no discussion, apparently.

"Look, you know that I have mail. I get mail every day and it's been more than a month. Where the hell is my mail?" I don't like her manner and now she doesn't like mine.

She stares at me without saying a word.

I yell, I slam my fist down on the counter, I curse at her. She stares at me, expressionless. Nothing I say is going to get her to turn around and walk back into that room and search for my mail.

"There's no mail. You can leave now." She turns her back on me and sits down at a desk. I hurl a couple more insults at her: she is lying, she is too lazy to go back and look for my mail. I say all this while staring at her back. "Goodbye," she calls over her shoulder.

I storm out of the post office.

A few days later I found out what happened to my mail.

The D.C. postal carriers had gotten so far behind in delivery that they were dumping mail into trucks that were parked behind the central post office. Hundreds of thousands of letters, bills, and packages were getting tossed into the semis. Most D.C. residents weren't affected; others wouldn't even notice that a letter wasn't delivered that week. In my case, since I happened to be gone for so long, they had apparently taken my entire pile and dumped it into the truck.

All this came out in a newspaper story. The head of the local post office was quoted as apologetic, vowed it would never happen again, and was appropriately remorseful. That didn't do me any good. I wanted my mail. How could I get it?

The head of the post office explained that the trucks were so jammed with mail that they couldn't go back now and deliver it all, because they would just fall hopelessly behind in delivering the current mail. He proposed a solution. Anyone who believed that their mail was tossed out could come down to the central post office and search the trucks.

Search the trucks? My mail was as good as buried. I had to let it go.

Then I thought back to the postal worker I had berated for not finding my mail. She had been right. There was no mail for me in her back room; it had never gotten there. There was nothing for her to find because it was buried in the back of a truck at the central office.

There was a message in this that went beyond my mail. There was something about her manner: the dismissiveness, the minimal communication, the detachment. I had witnessed my own teaching style. That was the very way I treated students in my classroom.

She had simply stated the facts, there was no need for discussion, no need to consider my opinion or how I "felt." She had turned her back on me without care. Mechanical, sterile, no wasted words, efficient.

I had looked in a mirror. But it would take years before that reflection sank in.

I made phone calls to the utilities and the credit card company and paid my last bill. My checkbook was still open on the table when I thought back to Johnson and Tanzania.

With some additional money, he could keep Anna and Susanna at school. Without the money, their education ends and they go back to a life in the bush.

No one asked me for the money; no one told me not to give it either. I was drawn into the battle, and I could choose to arm one side. Estomii or Johnson? Masai or the scientific modern world?

I picked up a pen and wrote a check to the Longido Secondary School. It wasn't because I cared about these people—Anna or Susanna or Johnson. Rather, I did it to validate my own point of view. Johnson was a practitioner of the scientific method. That, I believed, was my identity.

Then, I turned on my computer and wrote the story of Estomii, Johnson, and me for an educational journal. I laid it all out: my disregard for Estomii, my sympathy for Johnson, and how I could relate to his stiff teaching methods. I concluded the article explaining that I wrote a check that would keep Anna and Susanna in school, apart from their families. I thought the readers would understand my decision. I was wrong.

Readers found me self-absorbed, insensitive, and disconnected.

Cold and broken was the consensus.

I neither disagreed with those criticisms nor apologized. The fact is, they were accurate.

Self-absorbed? Yes, I admit it. That's why I let Pax climb down El Cap and mangle his feet, never offering him an assist.

Cold? Insensitive? I remember thinking at the time: what's wrong with that? Insensitivity can come in handy, depending on how you live your life. It was probably the very thing that fortified Warren Harding, kept him pursuing El Cap despite all odds being against him. And I knew from my own experience that being insensitive can get you back on your feet, even if you have a corkscrew break running down your fibula.

Disconnected? Certainly. And why not? I was independent. I wasn't connected to others and they weren't connected to me. The world was a place to play and work, nothing more.

Three Pillars

I had no intention of changing. I could even add a few more things to the list that I knew would never change, three pillars that formed my foundation.

Pillar #1: I would never get married.

Relationships were little more than ways to fill the evenings. I'm sure that the women I went out with all recognized this within a date or two. Fortunately, some of them were gracious enough to tolerate me for longer than that.

Pillar #2: I would never buy a house.

A home would create permanence. It would make me a fixed point on a map, pinned down and limited. That could only lead to complacency and, what I dreaded most, stagnation.

Pillar #3: I would never have kids.

Opting to have children was the ultimate limiting decision. In doing that, I would have to live for someone else and I had no intention of ever letting that happen.

And so I ignored what lessons there were to be learned from the comments of the readers of that educational journal. My teaching, my relationships, my identity were all challenged and I should have carried out a little self-reflection. But I didn't, because I didn't care. If I had concluded anything from writing that article, it was this: ignore the world and stay focused. I decided that I would never write about my travels again. I went back to the To Do List.

Over the next two years I would summit Mount Elbrus in Europe and Cerro Aconcagua in South America. I was moving through the list with efficiency, this time not forming ties with the local communities that could produce nothing but distractions.

I thought I knew who I was: confident in my attitude and foundation.

Then everything changed.

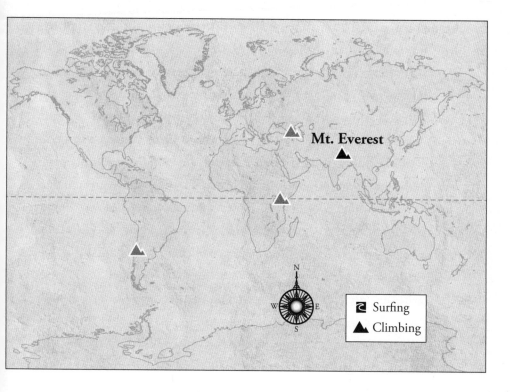

Mt. Everest

Surfing

Climbing

Chapter 4

THE AMULET

Most people probably expect the meaning of life to be housed in a remote monastery in the Himalayas, protected by an assembly of chanting monks. That's a reasonable expectation. After all, I'm told that's where I found it.

When I was on my way to the Base Camp of Everest, our

expedition passed the monastery of Thyangboche, the home of the Most Holy Rinpoche of the Khumbu.

The monastery is the stuff of legend. The monks believe that when the Buddha was circling the earth looking for a place to make his home, he saw a mountaintop that offered a view of the most majestic peaks on the planet. The site was irresistible and the Buddha came in for a landing. Like an inexperienced pilot, he came in too fast, heels hitting the granite mountaintop and bouncing him off the ground and down the mountainside. He rolled to a stop thousands of feet below on the valley floor. Rather than taking flight and trying again, this time with a better approach, he simply accepted his fate and made his home at the mountain's base.

Centuries later, monks claimed to find the very piece of granite where the Buddha's heels hit the mountaintop and they built the monastery of Thyangboche on that spot. As we walked up the ancient stone steps into the sanctuary, there in front of us was a bulge of granite with two deep six-inch-wide depressions, the imprints, the monks explained, of the Buddha's heels, his faulty landing gear.

We entered the private prayer room and, draped in a red robe, a counselor by his side, the Rinpoche sat cross-legged. With a face like soft brown Play-Doh, his heavy eyes staring out through large round glasses, he waved us in.

The Rinpoche has staying power. According to his followers' best estimates, he has had at least six reincarnations spanning three centuries, and he's been living at Thyangboche for most of the last one hundred years. As far as I can tell, he's spent most of that time sitting on a cushion.

We were there for a blessing, a ceremony that the locals, the Sherpas who were supporting our expedition, insisted must be done to insure the best possible outcome on the climb. We respectfully bowed our heads and the Rinpoche placed a silk scarf around each team member's neck.

The Amulet

It's not every day that you get to meet someone who's been meditating for three hundred years, and I realized I wanted to make the most of the opportunity. This was a chance to ask him the big question: what is the meaning of life? I didn't want to ask it so crudely, not in a hackneyed way that might make him roll his eyes and think I was clowning. So as the ceremony came to a close, I popped the question this way: "Can you give me an insight to keep in mind as I climb the mountain?"

Evidently, I breached protocol. In the century that the Rinpoche had been sitting on the cushion, no one had asked him a question. The Sherpas were stunned, embarrassed by me, the thickheaded Westerner.

The translator whispered my question to the Rinpoche, who paused in deliberation. Finally, he leaned into the ear of the translator and whispered a phrase. I prepared for an epiphany. The translator cleared his throat.

"He'll get back to you on that."

Three hundred years of deep reflection and I get a brush-off? There must have been some insight he could have offered. I would have settled for "buy low, sell high."

That evening, I heard rustling outside my tent. I pulled up the flap to find a young monk with a scarf-wrapped bundle from the Rinpoche. When I unfolded the scarf, I found an amulet, with the following letters freshly etched by the Rinpoche:

I stared down at the letters, for how long I don't know, but when I looked back up, the monk was gone and I sat alone in the tent.

The next morning I went around camp searching for someone who could translate it for me. Our expedition was populated by Sherpas, any one of whom could read it, I thought.

News of the amulet had spread across the camp and every Sherpa I walked up to would inexplicably cover his eyes and turn away.

I asked my Sherpa friend Pemba what was going on.

"This amulet is meant for you. It contains a powerful message, life meaning, and you must read it and keep it to yourself."

"That's fine, Pemba, but there's just one problem. I can't read it."

He stared back at me expressionless; he didn't see that as a problem. I tried again.

"The Rinpoche gave this to me and wanted me to read it. So, by helping me translate it, you would be fulfilling the wishes of the Rinpoche. Right?"

I doubt that Pemba was persuaded by my logic, more likely he was simply overcome with curiosity.

I unrolled my fingers, exposing the amulet in my palm, and Pemba dropped his chin down for a look.

"What does it say?"

"I don't know," Pemba responded.

"Who does?"

"Nobody. It is written in old language."

"What do you mean, 'nobody'? Obviously, the Rinpoche knows what it says. He wrote it."

"It is very, very old writing from scrolls," Pemba explained. "We can recite, but we don't know what it means."

The next day, Pemba took my amulet and sewed it up tight in a pouch woven from the fabric of a blessed scarf. He explained that I should wear it around my neck and not take it off, even if it itched. I obliged.

And so I arrived at the Base Camp of Mount Everest with an unreadable message hanging around my neck.

The Amulet

————

Everest is an expensive mountain to climb.

When I was planning to climb the mountain, in January of 2000, the cost of a permit to climb the south side—the Nepali side as opposed to the Tibetan side—was $10,000. On top of that expense was the cost of two months of food, additional high altitude gear, and bottled oxygen. There were also the considerable logistics of getting all of that gear where it needs to be: Base Camp, at an elevation of eighteen thousand feet, reachable only by foot.

Fortunately, I fell in with a team of climbers who had all the logistics worked out. Their expedition would not only climb the mountain but they had an associated mission to clean off the trash that had been accumulating ever since the first attempt to summit the peak more than a half century earlier. The high camps of Everest are inhospitable places and the last thing a climber worries about in a dicey situation is packing up the trash. Stoves, gas canisters, wind-torn tents, oxygen bottles, all of that litters the camps above twenty thousand feet.

In order to accomplish the cleanup mission, the expedition was vast, bigger than any expedition in the previous fifty years: thirteen Western climbers, twenty-five Sherpas assigned to the cleanup, and another twelve Sherpas assigned to the climb. An additional fifty porters and one hundred yaks would get the gear to Base Camp.

Despite its enormous size, the expedition team decided that they could accommodate a few more climbers and my friend and climbing partner Jim Williams was invited to join and he in turn invited me. And so, in early April of 2000, Jim and I flew to Nepal.

The team came up with several methods for covering the expenses of the effort. They advertised the "unique opportunity" that, for a modest price, an aspiring adventurer could trek "to Base Camp with real Everest climbers." Of course, that's as far as any trekker would be allowed to go. Once we got to Base Camp, we would turn the trekkers around and send them home where they belonged while we continued on with the climb.

Who would go for that? I thought. Why would someone want to trek along with climbers? I assumed no one would sign up. I was wrong. The team signed on fifty-three trekkers.

I didn't care much about the trekkers. I thought they were probably suckers for having fallen for the "unique opportunity" gimmick; they could have done the trek on their own and saved money. So I didn't want to be bothered by them; and I was sure they didn't want to be bothered by me. I didn't mingle; I had the mountain on my mind.

Fewer than half of the fifty-three trekkers managed to make it to Base Camp. Exhaustion or altitude sickness sidelined the rest of them on the way up. They were left at lower camps and villages, to be collected by the trek leader on her way back down the mountain.

When I walked into the mess tent the day we arrived at Base Camp, one of the trekkers, Gina Eppolito, was trying to corral our entire climbing team into circling up for a photo.

I hated the idea.

I don't own a camera, and never plan on owning one. Photographs break the moment; they interrupt the flow. Besides, I am not one of those people who look forward to the day that I can sit back in a rocking chair and flip through a photo album, the faded yellowing pictures warming my heart. Instead, I want to be planning my next adventure, even if, in my later years, it's nothing more than a card game.

Earlier on the trek I had overheard Gina talking about her hobby: pet photography. There were a half dozen other trekkers sitting around her, laughing with her at the story of a dog owner who demanded to pose beside his poodle.

"I told him the dog didn't want him in the shot," said Gina.

I interrupt the laughing with a question. "Why do you take pictures of dogs?"

"Why do you care?" she says.

I thought I was the one asking the question. "So the dog is still alive, right?"

No one is laughing now, they're all looking back and forth at Gina and me.

"Of course the dog is alive." She can't believe I just asked that. "Who asks for a picture with a dead dog?"

Just as I thought. "Well if the dog is alive, why does the guy need a picture? There's no point in looking at the picture; he can just look at the dog instead."

This was the first time I had spoken to any of the trekkers on the expedition. A minute ago they were laughing, now it's dead silent. I let the quiet settle in. I had made my point. No doubt, I thought, they now all see how silly pet photography is. As I walked away, the conversation started back up, too hushed for me to hear a clear word.

On the day she was corralling the climbers at Base Camp, I sat down for the photo. I remember being surly, annoyed, waiting to get it over with, simply accommodating her out of some sense of recognition that her check helped cover Base Camp expenses. I knew that after the photo was taken I would never see Gina Eppolito, or any of the trekkers, again.

It's a big world and what would be the odds of us ever bumping into each other again: one in a million? It wouldn't happen.

For the next few weeks we established our camps and acclimatized to the thin air, adhering to the mantra: "climb high, sleep low."

The best way to get accustomed to the lack of oxygen is to climb up a few thousand feet, sit, and breathe. Then, before nightfall, come back down to Base Camp and sleep in thicker air.

Days would begin before sunrise. Strapping on crampons, packs bursting with gear, the sky heavy with clouds, we would exit our tents and climb a few thousand feet to establish a higher camp.

By early May, the camps were all established, four of them, strung along the mountainside each one a few thousand feet higher in elevation than the last, loaded with the necessary provisions to allow one shot at the summit.

With the camps established, the waiting began.

Typically, the jet stream sits over the summit of Everest. You can actually see the stream, visible because of the snow it hurls from the summit, like smoke billowing off a chimney.

It's impossible to summit in the full force of the two-hundred-mile-per-hour jet stream. Instead, climbers wait for a weather window to open.

Every year, typically in mid-May, the monsoons will start building in the Indian Ocean and start moving northward. That motion pushes the jet stream off the mountain. The wind dies down then and the summit becomes accessible. But that window of opportunity is open only briefly because as the monsoon continues moving northward toward the Himalayas it turns into a blizzard and starts dumping heavy snows that are impossible to climb through.

That weather window—after the jet stream moves off the mountain, but before the blizzards settle in—typically lasts only a few days. So timing is crucial.

If climbers attempt the summit too soon, then they have to turn around because the jet stream hasn't completely moved off the mountain and the winds are still too strong. A climber on the fully exposed summit ridge would get blown off the mountain in the two-hundred-mile-per-hour gale. If climbers attempt the summit too late, then they will get hammered by a blizzard, pinned down in a half dozen feet of snow.

Weather predictions are no more certain in the Himalayas than they are anywhere else in the world. While our expedition had the most advanced communication tent on the mountain, we were still left guessing as to when was the best time to go for the summit.

Complicating the decision is a time lag. If everything goes smoothly, it typically takes three days to go from Base Camp to the summit. So weather forecasts have to be read with an eye toward the future, three days ahead. A forecast that may seem promising today may be a disaster at 10 P.M. two days later when you are strapping on your boots at Camp IV readying yourself for the summit.

Despite all our advanced technology at Base Camp, despite getting updated weather printouts every few hours, in the end we would simply be making a guess.

And so we waited, looking for things to do to fill the time.

One of the climbers had brought a copy of the 1999 version of *The Mummy*. One evening we had a movie night for all the climbers and Sherpas on the team.

The Sherpas had never seen a movie before. They also didn't have any idea of what a mummy was, or a desert, or a camel.

The Sherpas had spent their lives in the pastoral setting of the Himalayas, never having seen TV. On one cold night in May they took a seat in a tent and on a screen in front of them they witnessed skeletons emerging from walls, a gargantuan head of sand swept up from a desert floor, explosions, swarming beetles, a collapsing pyramid. And then, suddenly, it all came to an abrupt end with the two survivors kissing each other in the setting sun.

There was complete silence in the tent as the movie ended and the credits rolled up the screen. No clapping, no cheers. The Sherpas were in a state of shock.

One by one, the Sherpas stood up and quietly left the tent. The Sirdar, the head Sherpa, was the last to stand and before leaving the tent he turned to us and gave us his assessment.

"This is very strange love story." He shook his head and strolled out the tent into the crisp night air.

That was the only cultural exchange I would have with the Sherpas over the entire five weeks I was at Base Camp. I didn't ask about their educational system or consider ways they could improve their condition. I had been down that road and I was holding to the lesson I'd learned from that article I had written about Tanzania, Estomii, and Johnson: minimal interaction, focus on the climb.

By mid-May nearly all the teams on the mountain had already made their attempts to summit. So far, no one had been successful. No one had hit the weather window at the right time, and everyone was returning exhausted. They were packing up and going home. The mountain was emptying out.

At some point, you just have to take your shot, whether or not the weather appears to be cooperating. And so it was with our team. We folded up the forecast data, it no longer mattered. We had waited long enough; it was time to go for the summit. In the back of our minds, though it was left unsaid, we all knew that we would be climbing up into a storm.

You can smell in the morning air when a team begins its summit attempt. To bring luck to the climb, the Sherpas will burn branches of juniper trees on the morning a team leaves Base Camp for its three-day summit run. I've been smelling the morning pyre of other teams for the last two weeks. Now it is our time to burn some juniper.

As we pass the branches smoking in the makeshift altar I fill my lungs with the sweet-smelling smoke. This is often a spiritual moment for climbers who pause, perhaps bend a knee, say a prayer to invoke whatever blessings they can muster to ward off tragedy and bring safety and good luck to them and their team for the next forty-eight hours of hardship and toil.

It isn't a spiritual moment for me. As I pass the altar, I put on my headphones and spin up "Calm Like a Bomb" by Rage Against the Machine:

What ya say? What ya say? What ya say? What?
Calm like a bomb

Within a few minutes I'm out of camp and approaching the Khumbu Ice Fall. This will be the last time I will be going up the Ice Fall, thankfully.

Even though it sits far below the summit, the Ice Fall is the deadliest place on Everest. More than on any other spot on the mountain, climbers have died here, among the towering blocks of ice scattered like a thousand refrigerators air-dropped by a passing cargo plane.

A glacier isn't a static slab of ice. It is in motion, a river of ice slowly, very slowly, sliding down the side of the mountain. The glacier on the side of Everest is more than a quarter mile thick in spots and it is estimated to move a few millimeters a day.

The glacier descends smoothly from the summit until it reaches 22,000 feet, where there is a dramatic one-thousand-foot ledge. When the glacier reaches that point, as the massive sheet of ice slides forward, the ice hangs out over the ledge until it snaps from its own weight. Like a broken branch exposing shards of wood, the broken glacier leaves sharp, enormous, lethal slabs of ice scattered about the ledge, creating the Ice Fall.

The climber enters into the Ice Fall, surrounded by the towering multi-ton blocks of ice that have split off the glacier as it bends over the ledge. The blocks sway, tilt, tumble, and can crush a climber. Over a period of a week, the route up the Fall will change dramatically, shifting around newly formed walls and blocks. There is only one good way to manage the risk: move quickly. The less time spent in the Ice Fall the better.

I spend my first night of our summit run at Camp I, at the top of the Ice Fall. We had established the camp a month earlier and there is evidence of the glacier's motion over that time. The camp has moved, shifted with the sliding glacier, now further down the mountain from where we first set it up. New crevasses, fissures in the ice, have emerged. The camp is literally flowing down the mountain. This would be my last night overlooking the Ice Fall. I wouldn't miss it.

I know that for some climbers every bit of the route up Everest is memorable, every step is emotional, the very strain and punishment of arriving at a camp worthy of a lengthy dispatch home.

I understand that, and I recognize that those climbers are probably taking in their surroundings. I couldn't do that.

In my case, the route to the highest camp, Camp IV, at 26,000 feet, was uneventful. Certainly, things occurred between the morning I left the Ice Fall to when I arrived at Camp IV. In fact, only half our team made it up to Camp IV, the rest turning back in exhaustion and defeat. But I remember little of it.

For me, the deepest memories don't begin until that evening, when I awoke from a rest and pulled on a boot, readying myself for the summit.

My watch alarm wakes me at 10 P.M. and I tug my headlamp over my hat and twist the lens to switch on the beam. I shine the light up at the thermometer that dangles from the roof of the tent. Forty below zero.

Outside my tent flap are the last three thousand vertical feet of ice and granite that lie between me and the summit of Everest. It's time for the final push.

I had planned out exactly what I'd be wearing. I already have on my down suit and a thin pair of gloves. The rest is laid out along the tent wall or tucked deep in my sleeping bag to keep it warm: inch-thick boots, climbing harness, mitts, oxygen bottle, backpack. I would strap it all on in that order. I lift up out of my sleeping bag and grab a boot.

With a hand on each side of the boot, I pull up hard, pressing down firmly with my left foot, not sure what to expect.

My left leg can be a challenge; it has never been 100 percent since I broke my fibula, cleaving it into two in that rock climbing accident. This time, the leg slides neatly into place.

At 26,000 feet I have to pause for a few breaths before I lace up.

The second layer of the boot is also a tight fit. I slide in with a tug and pull the Velcro tight to fix it in place. The final layer is a Gore-Tex shell that keeps the boot windproof and waterproof. I wrap it around the boot and push down on the seal. Done.

I look down at my watch. It looks like it reads 10:30 P.M. That can't be right. It can't possibly be later than 10:05. I rub my thumb over the face of the watch thinking that some condensation is obscuring the numbers. It now reads 10:31 P.M.

I stare down in disbelief. It has just taken me a half hour to put on one boot.

Time has become taffy, stretched out beyond recognition. What I thought were mere seconds were actually, somehow, elongated into minutes. It is now clear, undeniable, that I am massively deteriorating, mentally and physically. Everest is tearing me down. The thin air is crushing me. I have to get this climb done as quickly as possible. I pull on the other boot, strap on the rest of my gear, and head out of the tent, up toward the summit.

Over the next few hours, I reach what climbers refer to as the Balcony, the gateway to the Everest ridgeline and one of the last patches of flat ground until the summit, 2,500 feet above. That would be my last restful moment for the next twenty hours.

The snow begins shortly after 5 A.M. I knew it was coming, every climber on the mountain that morning knew it was coming. The forecasts hadn't been good and the wind had been picking up for the last couple of hours, the sky looking heavy.

Within minutes the view in front of me is obscured by snow. I am just a few dozen feet below the South Summit, the false summit, a spot that rises up sharply, feeling like the peak only to drop back down, requiring the climber to make another push upward still hours away from the real summit.

As I climb higher, the clouds abruptly thin. I pull up a few more feet, onto the South Summit, and the clouds of the storm blow below me and I stand up in the full light of the morning. The storm is there, beneath me, raging, but I am a dozen feet above it all, looking out over a tranquil sun-filled sky. I can see Everest's summit ahead of me cutting up through the clouds, oblivious to the storm.

Some climbers who are reading this will understand what I did next; others may not. Without consideration, without any reflection or pause, I pushed on.

Of course, I had plenty of good reasons to turn around.

I had completely lost visual contact with my team. Some were ahead of me, some behind. Some, as I found out later, had already turned around, recognizing the dangers of climbing into a storm, accepting the end of their summit attempt and returning to Camp IV. As a result I was now climbing solo, uncomforted by the silhouette of a teammate, alone to decide, alone to slip and vanish without witness.

The storm would only get worse. In fact, just moments earlier I had radioed back to Base Camp to let them know my position and alert them to the fact that the weather was rapidly deteriorating. It turns out that the team at Base recorded my message and a year later, when a movie about the expedition aired on the National Geographic Channel, you hear my voice radioing these few desperate words: "It's complete whiteout conditions here. I can't see a damn thing and the team is totally spread out."

Then my radio goes silent.

The easy explanation for why I pushed ahead to the summit is that hypoxia, the lack of oxygen, was clouding my judgment and that now, in the rich air of sea level, I can recognize the foolishness of my decision and admit that the right thing to do at that moment was turn around.

But no.

In hindsight, even knowing now that a crisis was about to ensue, I still would not have done it differently.

I dropped down off the South Summit and back into the storm, crossing the knife edge without incident. With the storm worsening, I knew that it would present a challenge on my way back, but for now I would focus on the summit, just a hundred feet above me.

The final challenge to reaching the summit is the Hillary Step, forty feet of near-vertical granite with pockets of deep snow.

I have been on climbs before when I'm near a summit, having just made what I thought was the final big push, only to discover when I come up over the ledge that I still have another more exhausting haul to go. It can be dispiriting to confront another challenge when you are already so depleted.

But when I stood at the base of the Hillary Step, I didn't feel despair or frustration. I wasn't distraught, or crushed. I didn't need to pause and refocus my energy. Instead, I was thrilled.

———

I am taking deep rasping breaths, satisfied, on my knees at the summit of Mount Everest.

For the last several hours I've been climbing alone, no one in sight. Now I can see a climber rising up over the ridge. He walks up beside me and drops down in the snow.

I haven't radioed Base Camp since just before the South Summit. I have no idea how long ago that was, perhaps hours. I click on the power and give Base the news.

"This is Slake. I'm on the summit." I couldn't have chosen duller words.

Cheers erupt from the radio.

They are miles away, separated by storm, crevasse, and rock. They couldn't reach me by any means no matter their desire or wealth. I couldn't be more detached. Yet I hear their voices and realize I couldn't be more connected.

This stranger on the summit with me has no radio. I believe he is looking at me, though it's impossible to tell through his tinted goggles.

I decide to give him the chance to experience what I'm feeling: a sense of connection despite our utterly desperate circumstances. I hand him the radio. I don't even know what language he will speak.

He pushes down on the button and says a few soft words in what I suspect is Russian.

He releases the button and all we hear is static. I imagine that the team at Base is baffled. The Russian isn't a member of our expedition. Our team has no attachment to him, no reason for celebration.

Cheers erupt again from the radio.

They know all they need to know. This Russian is on the summit, and like any other climber who has struggled through the storm to get to this point, he deserves his moment of triumph.

I take the radio from his hand and make one last transmission from the summit.

"I'm on my way down."

The shouts of good luck fade as I spin down the knob and click off the radio. I have been on this mountain for fifty-four days and I spent just two minutes on the summit.

I stand up and begin my trip home.

This is the last place on Earth you would expect a fork in the road. Yet, here it is, at 29,029 feet, the highest point on the planet, and I'm heading in the opposite direction from the Russian. He turns north, heading down to Tibet, and within a few moments his silhouette vanishes behind a curtain of snow. I turn south, toward Nepal, into the teeth of the storm.

I am facing a growing list of problems.

First of all, I am descending into a blizzard alone. Over the last two hours our climbing team has gotten completely spread out along the southeast ridge and we've lost contact as our radios have become ineffective amid the twists and turns of Everest's summit.

At most, there is roughly thirty feet of visibility. The blizzard is so severe that the ridgeline blurs into the background of falling snow. Under ordinary circumstances I could easily deal with that. But here it won't be easy because somewhere up ahead the ridgeline narrows to just a bit wider than my boot and there is a four-thousand-foot drop-off on either side.

Making matters worse is the cornice of snow that hangs over that narrow ridgeline, creating an illusion that the path is a few feet wider than it actually is. If I place a foot on the snow cornice instead of the rock of the ridgeline, I'll plunge through, falling nearly a mile down the mountainside.

The good news is that there is shelter ahead; the bad news is that it's on the other side of that corniced knife edge and still hours away.

The tracks I left coming up to the summit just a few minutes ago have been scrubbed away by the wind and snow, but the direction I need to go is still obvious—even in a blizzard, down is still apparent when you're standing on the highest point on Earth.

I take in a big draw of air from my oxygen tank and the rasp is just audible over the thirty-mile-per-hour wind. With that, it's time to go to work.

I take my first step down the mountain and immediately feel depleted. Adrenaline is a direction-sensitive stimulant. My body has been producing gallons of it since I set out for the summit at midnight, but the moment I turned around to go back down the spigot went dry. I have felt this on every climb I have ever done and other climbers tell me they experience the same thing: adrenaline on the way up, an empty tank on the way down.

These are the moments when I have my greatest focus. It's not that my mind is sharp; at this altitude, with this level of fatigue, I know that my mind is as thick as timber. And it's not that I'm broadly aware of my circumstances. In fact, now, at this moment, my world has become astonishingly small. It no longer consists of friends and family. My hometown, the smell of coffee, the push and hustle of my job, the last book I read—all of that is distant and forgotten.

The only thing that exists in my life right now is the square foot of snow directly in front of me where I will plant my next step. I can sense that spot with absolute clarity. I can see the bend of the snow, feel the weight of the falling flakes, sense the flakes settle on the ridge creating a new contour. The shadows and folds of a small patch of snow and rock are my entire world now.

I guide my foot to the spot I've been staring at and the metal claws of my crampon punch through the snow, gripping and taking my weight as I lean forward sinking deep into fresh powder. I take in three breaths before I'm ready for another step. I pull my boot out of the foot-deep hole of snow and plod forward. This descent is happening in slow motion, like walking through a vat of molasses.

My speed is limited by the intense fatigue and the layers of clothes I'm wearing to weather the twenty-below-zero temperature. I'm encased in a down suit, hands sealed in thick gloves, my face layered in a mask and goggles. Two days from now, when I'm back in Base Camp, I will discover that there was a small gap in all that wrapping. A square of flesh on my cheek, no bigger than a postage stamp, was exposed to the subzero chill. The result is a patch of thick blackened skin, crisped like a burnt marshmallow. It takes months for the skin to return but it forever remains sensitive to the cold.

As I move slowly down the mountain I see three figures ahead of me, barely visible in the blizzard. They stand no more than thirty feet away, but their movements are obscured in the swirling snow. With the wind howling, I can't hear a word they are saying although it is clear they are trying to communicate. Then, suddenly, inexplicably, one of them sits down. The other two stand above him, hovering. They speak for a few more moments, turn, and then continue on down the mountain and out of sight.

At this altitude, in this weather, sitting can mean only one thing. Whoever just sat down has decided to die. The climbers who are walking away have chosen to let that happen.

How could those two climbers walk away? Over the next few hours, my understanding of that moment would turn inside out.

I don't know how I missed seeing him before, but another climber suddenly becomes visible and approaches the sitting climber. As I approach, I realize that I know them both. Jim Williams, my climbing partner from Wyoming, is standing above the sitting climber, Ang Nima, a Sherpa guide from Nepal.

Despite having vastly different starting points, our personal stories have now converged in a subzero whiteout on the summit ridge of Everest. Staring at each other in silence, we know that however this dilemma spins out, this moment will forever shape us.

I break the silence. "Ang Nima, you have to get up; you have to get on your feet."

"No, this is not necessary. Everything is fine," Ang Nima responds. There is no desperation in his voice. Instead, there is serenity, a delicacy. Listening to him you would think we were casually reminiscing over beers or lounging in a meadow on a warm summer evening.

Jim's voice crackles with a reminder that the situation is desperate. "If you sit, you will die. You have to keep moving."

"I will stay. You go."

Ang Nima's mind must be in a fog.

The mind is an inventive creature. At sea level in the comfort of your own home you can let it have free range and delight in its mischief. But the summit of Everest is not the place for mischief. This is where your brain tells you that you're tired, that sitting for a moment will revive you, that all you need is a short rest to restart your failing engine. Those are the tantalizing whispers of Odysseus's Sirens and to listen to those voices is to be lured to your death.

Jim is shouting now, his voice barely audible over the sound of the screaming wind. "Get up now." Each word is spoken like a hammer stroke trying to break through the frozen crystals of Ang Nima's mind and bring back his focus.

"I will be fine. Go. I will be back."

He'll be back? And then I realize that Ang Nima isn't being lulled into complacency. Instead, he has clarity; he has thought this through and his mind is settled. In fact, he has a reason to be content with his decision.

What does it take to decide to sit down and die, to willingly accept the end? In the United States, the vast majority of our lifetime health costs will be spent in the last two months of our lives in a desperate effort to scrape out one more day, one more minute. We don't accept the end so easily.

Ang Nima lives in a different world. As he sits in the snow, reflecting back on his days, he is reassured by one simple fact: he is a good man. That, to him, can mean only one thing. He will be reincarnated into a life no worse than what he has had. His conclusion, then, is that he can be calm amid the chaos. Buddhism is his universal health coverage.

That belief also explains how his Sherpa friends could walk away and leave him sitting in the snow. They know Ang Nima; they know what a good man he is. Perhaps they envy him a little because he may return for an even better life. They can walk on with a clear conscience. All three are content.

Reincarnation is a wonderfully serene worldview. But I don't buy it. When people die, they are gone. I learned that as a child.

Ang Nima believes that he is coming back; I am certain that he is not. Our worldviews are about to have a smackdown.

To Nima's credit, his view is shaped by two millennia of accumulated Buddhist teachings while my view is informed by merely a few centuries of advanced scientific experimentation and hypothesis. On the other hand, if Nima is wrong and I am right, then he is throwing away the one and only chance he has on this planet. With that, I decide that we must intervene. Jim is of the same mind. The only question is: what can we do?

We are silent once again as Jim and I consider the situation. The only sound is the screaming wind that keeps the snow whipping around us like a thick white cyclone. It is lifeless up here, as inhospitable as the dark side of the moon. No animal, no plant, nothing can survive here. This is not a place to linger; from the moment you leave the summit you are in a constant state of escape. Nima now risks becoming a permanent resident, joining more than a hundred other climbers who are frozen into this desolate mountainside.

We can't carry Ang Nima down. At this altitude, under these circumstances, it will be hard enough just managing our own body weight.

There is no point in radioing for help because no one would be able to get here in time.

There is only one course of action. It carries risk, but Nima's death is certain if we do nothing.

Some high altitude climbers carry two emergency drugs: dexamethasone and dextroamphetamine. That latter drug has a familiar street name: speed. These drugs weren't designed by the pharmaceutical industry to aid climbers; climbers just happened to discover the utility of these drugs in pulling out of dire situations such as this. Consequently, there is no guidance on dosage. If administered in the right amount, the dex cocktail can get a climber back up on his feet and home. If administered in the wrong proportions, the climber will never see home again.

Jim has dex tucked away in an inside pocket of his down suit. But there is one significant problem: Nima will refuse it. He has made his decision and is sitting passively, waiting for us to leave. With no climbers behind us on the mountain, it would be Nima's final goodbye.

All climbers have quirks, odd habits that keep us paced and confidently in the moment. I know a climber who brings a tiny stuffed bear on every expedition. I blast *Rage Against the Machine* on my music player when I start an ascent. And Jim, unlike any other climber I've known, carries hot tea in a small narrow thermos on summit days.

"Nima, let's share a cup of tea," Jim suggests.

Nima nods his agreement. No self-respecting Sherpa can refuse a cup of tea.

With his back turned to the wind Jim pours tea into the thermos lid, crushes some dex pills, and then tosses the powder into the cup. Steam from the cup spirals up into the wind as Nima drinks the tea.

What's done is done. The dose will either improve the situation or accelerate its decline. The outcome will be clear within a half hour as the drugs take effect. Jim decides to stay; either he will provide Nima a few final words of comfort or give Nima a hand and lift him to his feet. I continue on down the mountain expecting that one way or the other, the worst is now behind us. I am wrong.

At sea level, the brain tends to have a strong grip on reality. The world presents us with a situation or an image, and our synapses fire, neurons transmit, and signals race through the internal wiring of our skull creating an understanding. When the system works smoothly, we sense things as they are: hot is hot, cold is cold, and we only see two people on a mountain when there are only two people on a mountain. We don't hear dead people speak.

Oxygen is the lubricant that keeps the brain operating as it should; blood is the vehicle that transports the oxygen around to the various needy organs. Every organ wants a share of the blood, but the body prioritizes to make sure that the most critical needs are met first. In fact, without our even realizing it, the body operates under its own Golden Rule: keep oxygen flowing to the brain, everything else is bonus. Consequently, as a climber goes up in altitude into thinner and thinner air, the body monitors oxygen needs, reroutes blood flow, and flips system controls like a train switchman.

First, your body automatically ramps up your breathing rate as you go up in altitude. By the time a climber reaches Base Camp on

Everest, at eighteen thousand feet, the respiratory rate has roughly tripled. If you were taking a breath every ten seconds at sea level, then you'll be sucking in a breath every three seconds at Base. The impact on the metabolism is striking. If all you did all day long was sit in your tent at Base Camp doing absolutely nothing but breathe, you would still burn about three thousand calories a day. Forget about the Atkins Diet or spending hours on the elliptical machine—planting your butt at Everest Base Camp is the world's most effective weight loss program.

Thankfully, our body carefully monitors our breathing rate, even when we don't. If your body relaxes too much while you're sleeping and your breathing rate slips too low to satisfy the Golden Rule, then your body will snap you awake with a sharp spasmic gasp. Base Camp echoes with the sound of sudden rasping inhales throughout the night.

As a climber goes higher, the body begins to take more drastic measures to compensate for the thinning air. To preserve as much oxygen as possible for the brain, blood flow to the extremities becomes more limited. Fingers and toes start to go numb, making them dangerously susceptible to frostbite.

As a climber goes up even higher in altitude, into the so-called death zone, the dangerously thin air above 26,000 feet, there is so little oxygen available that the body makes a desperate decision: it cuts off the digestive system. The body can no longer afford to direct oxygen to the stomach to help digest food because that would divert what precious little oxygen is available away from the brain. The body will retch back up anything the climber tries to eat, even if it's as small as an M&M.

The consequence of shutting down the digestive system is, of course, that the body can no longer take in any calories. Lacking an external fuel source, the body has no choice but to turn on itself. It now fuels itself by burning its own muscle—the very muscle needed to climb the mountain—at a rate of about two pounds per hour.

The climber's body is now in total collapse. The respiratory system is working way beyond its tolerance at roughly four times above normal; the circulatory system is pumping at only 30 percent capacity; the digestive system has completely shut down; and the muscular system is eating away at itself. In short, the body is dying. Rapidly.

Up to this point the body has done an admirable job of prioritizing, rerouting blood, stealing from other systems to keep blood flowing to the brain. But if a climber chooses to continue to go up in altitude, then there are no more options left; the brain starts to massively erode. To stave off that decay, many climbers carry a tank of supplemental oxygen.

Supplemental oxygen for climbers doesn't operate like air tanks for SCUBA divers. SCUBA breathing systems are self-contained; climbing systems are not. Instead, a climber's tank is attached to a thin hose that flows a bit of extra oxygen just below the nose, enriching the ambient air by just a touch. The rule of thumb is that every liter per minute of flow from the tank will enrich each breath with the oxygen level equivalent to the air about one thousand feet lower in altitude.

Every climber who chooses to carry supplemental oxygen now considers two questions. How many tanks should I bring? How high of a flow rate can I set on the tank? The answers require trade-offs. If a climber brings more tanks, then a higher flow rate can be set and less deterioration results. But, and there is always a but, each tank adds weight that will slow the climber down.

All the climbers on our team brought two tanks and set their flow rate to two liters per minute. At that rate, climbers at the 29,029-foot-high summit of Everest will be breathing air as if they were at 27,029 feet. That doesn't sound like much of a difference, and for some climbers it's not enough.

Many climbers can't function at a low flow rate. Others set a higher flow rate in order to keep them more nimble, but they miscalculate the length of time it will take them to summit and their tanks run out. In either case, the inevitable consequence is that the brain doesn't get enough oxygen; the grip on reality goes slack, the mind drifts. However, the mind doesn't stop sending signals; instead it starts inventing its own tales. Making this even worse is that the climber doesn't even know that the deterioration is occurring.

I know all this, because I saw it unfold in front of me.

As I made my way down the southeast ridge of Everest, with Ang Nima and Jim Williams now a few hundred feet above me, I saw a climber from our team, Bob Clemey, on his knees, gloves at his side, with his bare hands delicately gliding over the surface of the snow.

Depleted and needing warmth, Clemey saw with absolute clarity that a rock protruding from the snow was glowing red hot. He realized that lava from the very core of the earth was lifted up to the surface of Everest and was heating that rock. So he stripped off his gloves and began warming his hands over the rock like it was a campfire.

In reality, there was no glowing red rock, no lava. There was just a climber with bare hands frozen as solid as clubs, fingers gripping snow in a twenty-below-zero blizzard.

Clemey's oxygen tanks were drained. There was no way of knowing how long he had been there or when he had run out of oxygen.

Sometimes, desperate moments are punctuated with relief. As I stood staring in shock at Clemey's condition, Ang Nima passed us by.

Jim later told me that the tea delivered a quick effect. Within minutes, Nima was back up on his feet, supported by Jim's steadying hand. A half hour later, with the drugs revitalizing his depleted body, Nima was supercharged: "Jim, why are we moving so slow? If we keep going slow we will get cold." Jim let go of the reins: "If you can go faster, do it. Get to camp as fast as you can." Nima surged ahead.

At the pace Nima was moving he would be back in high camp in a few hours. One problem was solved as the next one developed.

Within a few minutes Jim approached and for the second time that day we found ourselves standing beside a climber in a desperate situation. This time, the dex cocktail wouldn't solve the problem. Clemey needed a different drug; he needed oxygen. He could move, slowly, and it seemed possible that if he had someone watching his steps he could make his way back to camp. But for that to happen, he needed to get oxygen to his brain and get a grip on reality so he could navigate his circumstances.

The solution to this dilemma was obvious. Two of us had oxygen in our tanks, one of us didn't, and the one who didn't needed it. Something had to give.

High altitude has a way of stripping away all pleasantries. No one is on their best behavior. Up here, it's hard enough to survive, let alone sacrifice. We are all emotionally raw and the result is that when we are faced with moments like this, we discover whether we are a good person or a bad person. There is no better mirror to a climber's soul than his reflection in the goggles of a stricken climber.

"Clemey, take my oxygen tank," Jim said.

Those are the five most powerful words that I have ever heard. That offer is still the most pure, selfless act I have ever witnessed.

Clemey didn't hesitate; neither did Jim. We lifted the tank off Jim's back and attached it to Clemey. Jim then radioed down to high camp to see if there was someone who could get a spare oxygen tank up to where we were.

Within minutes, Clemey was back on his feet and Jim dropped down into the snow where Clemey had been. Jim was fully aware of the risks of sitting, but good news got radioed back from camp. There was one climber who didn't go for the summit that day who had the energy to climb up and deliver a bottle. Jim would stay put until the oxygen arrived.

Clemey needed to descend immediately; his fingers were already severely frostbitten and any more time at this altitude would inflict even more irreversible damage. I would help Clemey descend by making a foot trail in the snow for him. It would be slowgoing. We would be in the death zone for several more hours, for longer than was safe.

"See you soon, Jim," I said to my teammate, blizzard still raging.

"You will. I'll get back to camp, no problems." His words were assured. The underlying message was clear: stop thinking about me and get back to punching through this storm.

Clemey and I turned back into the blizzard and started descending. Two of us were now walking away from a sitting climber. Just a few hours earlier I had witnessed precisely this situation in disbelief when two Sherpas walked away from Ang Nima. Now I was walking away. My only comfort was my confidence that Jim would get through this; I was certain I would see him again back at camp.

Clemey followed close behind me as we worked our way down the mountain and through the pounding snow. The pace was slow, with Clemey placing his boot in each step I left behind. We looked no more than a few feet ahead of us; that was our world. I couldn't tell you how much time passed; I can't recall the terrain, my thoughts, the mood, nothing. Time simply passed, and with one slow step at a time we moved forward.

We made it down to the Balcony, just a thousand vertical feet above Camp IV, our highest camp on the mountain. We managed to get to this point without stress or calamity. And as we stopped to take a breather, for the first time in hours I became aware of my surroundings. The world began taking shape again.

Stars were emerging from behind the last wisps of the passing storm. The blizzard had probably been easing for the last hour, but I had no recollection of that either.

With stars coming up it was getting late. Nearly twenty-four hours must have passed since we had left from Camp IV for the summit. That meant it was at least ten hours later than when we had planned to get back and hours longer than anyone should be up in the death zone.

A climber was clearly visible below me, approaching the Balcony where we were resting. Who would be coming up to the ridge at this hour? Then it clicked. As the Sherpa nodded and went by me, I saw in his backpack the spare tanks of oxygen, Jim's lifeline. With the skies clearing, Jim would get oxygen within an hour or two. He would make it back and so would we.

Clemey's hands were like blocks of ice. In the end, he would lose every fingertip, down to the top knuckle, but he would make it home.

There was a fixed line below us, a series of ropes pinned into the ice. We clipped in and descended to camp.

Base Camp is an oasis, a place to rest knowing that survival is assured. And it is here, after a summit bid, that climbers first start reflecting on the climb. They bask in summits, reconstruct the terrors, or assign blame and disperse amid regrets.

It was at Base Camp that Clemey revealed that he had another hallucination as we were coming off the summit ridge. He saw, again with absolute clarity, that there was an ice cream stand just below the Balcony where we had paused to rest. He could also see that there was a vendor offering the ice cream. If we weren't in a hurry, Clemey told us, he would have stopped to buy a double-scoop cone.

It turns out there was someone precisely where Clemey had seen the ice cream vendor. It was a body, frozen into the ice. Clemey's hypoxic mind had built a hallucination around the body of Scott Fischer, a climber who died in a storm in 1996 that was detailed in Jon Krakauer's *Into Thin Air*.

And how clear was my mind? At that altitude, it's impossible to have total recall. But burned deep into my memory was that moment when I looked down at Ang Nima sitting passively in the snow. The lesson I drew when I was reliving it all in Base Camp was this: if your religion lets you sit down in the snow and die, you need a new religion.

I operated under a straightforward principle.

Climb, *to the last breath*. Never yield. No sitting down to die. Always, *to the last breath*.

Of course, the Sherpas drew a different lesson. Our survival had nothing to do with the keen decisions of Jim Williams or the eventual easing of the storm. No, they attributed our survival to that amulet. According to them, the amulet the Rinpoche gave me on our way up to Base Camp was etched with the meaning of life. It had juice; it provided protection.

My twenty years of experience as a physicist made me confident that events had concrete explanations. It wasn't the bit of wood hanging around my neck that lifted a sitting climber out of the snow or cleared the hypoxic mind of another. When I returned to the United States I tossed the amulet into a drawer and forgot about it.

It would take surviving another entanglement, deep in the jungles of Indonesia, before I would begin to relax my scientific need for explanation and regard that amulet as something more than a few letters etched onto a piece of wood. It would be nearly a decade and a journey spanning six more continents, four oceans, tens of thousands more miles, and a half dozen improbable events before I would decode the meaning of the amulet.

There were scores of messages on my answering machine when I got back home. I jumped ahead and played the last one.

"Congratulations on your summit. You might remember me, I'm Gina Eppolito, one of the trekkers on your expedition. If you want to celebrate over a dinner, give me a call. I live in Washington, D.C., in Tenleytown."

I traveled halfway around the world and met someone who lived just three Metro stops away from me? How unlikely was that? I called her back; I wanted to go out, at least once, just to verify the odds.

I'm sitting at the bar in Cactus Cantina, waiting for her to show up, reading a magazine I'd picked up on my way here. A friend recommended I read an article about how altitude has the same effect on the brain as drinking beer. It's telling me that high camp on Everest would be like drinking a six-pack.

"What are you reading?"

I turn away from the magazine and see Gina Eppolito for the first time at sea level, in street clothes instead of a parka. "It's an article about beer and climbing." I shut the magazine and notice her staring at the cover.

I look down at it. When I pulled the magazine off the rack I hadn't looked carefully. The woman on the cover is barely clothed, bursting out of her swimsuit.

"You read *Maxim*?" Gina asks.

"I did today," and I push the magazine aside.

"Hmmm." She changes the subject and points down at my sandals while we walk to our table. "Why are some of your toenails black?"

"Frostbite. It took me a bit longer to get down the mountain than I expected." Over the next few months I would get so tired of answering that I would paint all my toenails a deep blue. No one asked the question after that.

It became clear as we talked that her life was so different from mine that we would never have met in D.C. We didn't go to the same shows, or bars, or restaurants. We didn't belong to the same gym. We didn't have any friends in common. We would never have met in any of the ways people typically meet in a city. Our paths would never have crossed if she hadn't been on my trek on Everest.

I thought through just how unlikely that was.

Roughly ten thousand people went on treks in the Everest region that year, and we took fifty-three of them on our expedition. Gina could have gone on any one of those other organized treks. The odds of her being on mine were about 1 in 200.

What were the odds of her living in Washington, D.C.? She worked for American Airlines so she had a portable career and could live anywhere. She wanted to live in a city, but not one that was too small, at least 100,000 people. That meant that the odds of her picking D.C. were about 1 in 300. She had decided before she left on the Everest trek that when she returned, she would pack up and move to another city, her curiosity about D.C. fully satisfied.

There are plenty of neighborhoods in D.C., so the fact that she happened to live three Metro stops away from me were about 1 in 20.

Putting that all together, the odds of it happening were:

$$\left(\frac{1}{200}\right) \times \left(\frac{1}{300}\right) \times \left(\frac{1}{20}\right) \Rightarrow 1 \text{ in } 1,200,000$$

Remarkable. Less than a one-in-a-million chance. The coincidence was extraordinary; the odds of meeting on Everest and then connecting in Washington, D.C., were vanishingly small.

We walked out of the restaurant and I asked about seeing each other again.

"I'm leaving on a trip," Gina said, staring back at me, her interest impossible to read.

That was a familiar line, I said it dozens of times myself. I would say it again now.

"I'm leaving for Antarctica. Let's talk when we both get back to town."

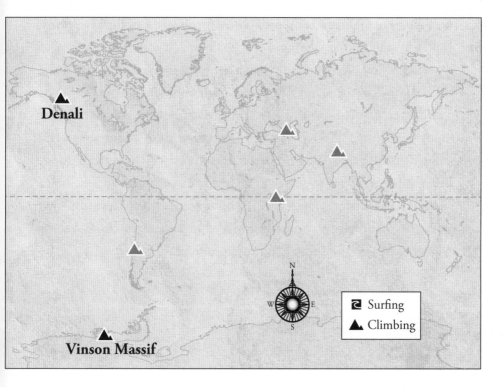

Chapter 5

COLD AND BROKEN

If a walrus had wings, it would fly like a Hercules C-130 cargo plane.

The plane lumbers through the air, propellers dragging its heavy load forward. You can feel the struggle in the cargo bay where the payload sways, the fuselage rattles as if the rivets will explode, the vibrations of the floor work through your toes up into your spine, and the four engines scream so loud that you need earplugs as thick as bullets just to muffle the sound to a low roar.

For the last three hours I've been confined in a seat that flips down from the wall of the plane. The plane's vibrations are shaking my bones; I'm past aching and we still have two more hours to go. We're riding along with cargo that's being delivered to a camp about a hundred miles deep into the manta ray–shaped continent of Antarctica. Among other things, the camp serves as a depot to stockpile supplies, some of which will then be taken further along to the South Pole itself. We won't be going all the way to the Pole; we're here to climb Vinson Massif, the highest mountain on the continent.

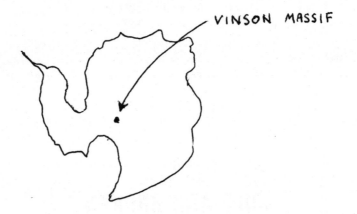

The remoteness of Antarctica can be measured in the price of a barrel of oil. A barrel that costs $40 in Santiago, Chile, costs $400 at the depot, and costs $4,000 at the South Pole. The increase scales with the cost of transport, and transport is pricey; the cost of spinning the propellers on a Hercules is roughly $10,000 per hour. We could never afford to book this flight on our own, and that's why we're traveling with a load of goods headed for the depot.

Sitting across from me is Jim Williams. Serene, head rolled back against the fuselage, he is inconceivably restful, looking like he could keep calm through any storm. In fact, he can. He did just that on our last climb, Mount Everest. That was just six months ago, and this mountain will be item #5 on my eleven-item climbing and surfing list.

There is no runway in Antarctica, but over the years of flying here, pilots have identified a long thick strip of ice that can handle the bulk of a Hercules.

The plane rolls to a stop and with a grinding of gears the back panel of the plane begins to slowly drop down onto the ice, forming a ramp off the cargo bay. As we watch the door swing down, inch by inch, light starts to fill the bay. Before we can see the continent, we can feel it. A subzero wind blows into the hold, and we take in our first lungful of chill Antarctic air. I exhale in a thick, visible cloud.

Antarctica's history is replete with tales of disaster, desperation, and triumph.

The first documented spotting of Antarctica was from the bow of a boat, in 1820. This was the one and only time in recorded history that a continent was truly discovered. There were no indigenous tribes here, no nomads who had passed through first. There is good reason for that, of course. The continent is utterly uninhabitable; there is nothing here that could sustain life: no fuel, no food, and despite having the largest amount of freshwater in the world, there isn't a drop readily available—it is all frozen up in mile-thick ice.

That glimpse of Antarctica in 1820 turned out to be the safest way to explore the continent: at a distance. Over the next century the continent brought misery to most anyone who traveled here. Just two years later, the first group of travelers spent a winter here. Not by choice, but due to shipwreck.

It wasn't until 1902 that a group would travel here with the intent of planting a flag at the South Pole. The Pole had been part of the public imagination for decades, but, like all expeditions, no team could hope to be successful until they solved the grueling logistics of pushing hundreds of pounds of gear and food across a thousand miles of ice.

The first attempt failed. The team, led by Robert Falcon Scott and Ernest Shackleton, pressed on through the subzero temperatures until they were overcome by snow blindness, frostbite, and scurvy. They turned back, still hundreds of miles short of the Pole.

Like customers in a ticket line, more expeditions followed, one after the other, often meeting with calamity. These expeditions weren't motivated by the possibility of wealth; this wasn't like Columbus being dispatched from Spain in the hopes that he would bring riches back to the kingdom.

Antarctica had no gold or coffee, no spices or beads. It offered only one thing: a story. No matter the characters or narrator, Antarctica always provided a tale of adventure about dog sleds, frostbite, and thinning rations, guaranteed to end in either tragedy or glory. Every nation that supported an expedition wanted that story to climax with their countryman's boot touching the South Pole first. They wanted to boast that it was the grit and will born out of the soil of their great nation that allowed the explorer to triumph over the calamities that the Pole was sure to deliver.

Robert Scott desperately wanted that story to be his to tell; he had to reach the Pole first. Buoyed by completely unfounded determination, he returned to Antarctica less than ten years after his previous failed expedition.

Like me, he too would step onto the continent and exhale in a thick, visible cloud and look out over the vast sheet of ice with confidence, a goal clearly fixed in his mind.

Scott's story would end in utter disaster. And his ultimate fate, his final desperate minutes, would lead to a turning point in my life.

Cold and Broken

———

The back bay of the Hercules rattles down onto the ice and I take my first step onto the continent. The first thing I see is completely unexpected, bizarre, like staring in a mirror and seeing someone else's reflection. Here, at the most lifeless, desolate, frigid place on the planet, where there is no possibility of warfare, there standing in front of me, is a Chilean soldier.

Who could he possibly be planning to shoot? Who is his enemy here? As it turns out, nowhere on the planet, no matter how desolate, is beyond politics.

"Chile thinks there might be something worth owning here," scoffs one of the Hercules pilots.

The Antarctic Treaty commits that no country will claim territory on the continent of Antarctica. Instead, the continent is recognized by most countries as a natural reserve, devoted to peace and science. There are detractors. Despite being an original signatory of the treaty, Chile now claims territory in Antarctica, and apparently they go to extremes to let the world know.

"I hear Chile flies pregnant women down here to give birth and claim citizenship," the pilot explains to me.

That could be a myth, but it's not hard to believe when you see their soldiers wandering around this desolate ice sheet. This has to be the most thankless assignment in Chile. These soldiers probably joined up hoping for a posting in sunny Santiago, but after one unshined boot or a sloppy salute they ended up in this frigid wasteland. Then again, I'm here by choice, and that probably is just as surprising to them.

Our stop here is brief. We swing on our packs, and start hauling out our duffel bags jammed full of supplies. Our next step is to go still deeper into the continent to a location with a patch of ice that is too short and narrow for the Hercules to reach. We'll get there by a Twin Otter, the four-seat prop plane that serves like a taxi to glacier climbers the world over.

Two hours later, the Twin Otter's skis glide to a stop in the snow and we climb out of the cabin onto the glacier at the foot of Vinson Massif.

"I'll be back in five days, if the weather's good," the pilot shouts over the hammering of the engine.

He climbs back into the Otter and rotates its nose to face the snow that he just flattened with his landing skis. His back presses against the seat as the plane accelerates, rises up into the sky, and drifts out of sight.

This remote continent has become even more desolate now. There are no soldiers, no planes or pilots, no other tracks in the snow but ours. With no possibility of a rescue in the event of a calamity, we now have minimal margin for error.

I look down at my watch and realize that time no longer has any meaning. The sun never sets during the Antarctic summer, daytime is endless, and hours can pass without consequence.

In fact, Antarctica is a massive sensory deprivation tank. There is almost nothing for the senses to work with here. I scroll through my senses, searching for something, anything, for them to grasp on to:

Smell

There is no scent here. There is no smell of fresh-cut grass, no aromatic flower or waft from a neighbor's barbeque. The ground that could support vegetation or a grill is buried under a mile of dense, odorless ice.

Cold and Broken

Sound

The glacier is quiet, lifeless. Barks, chirps, a car horn, the cool tone of a muted trumpet, the whisper of a friend in a darkened movie theater, all of that is the sound of another, distant continent. Here there is silence—penetrating, evident, and heavy.

Sight

It is white, everywhere. The ice, snow, and sky all blend together in a blank colorless canvas. There isn't even a nighttime to offer some variety. The sun sits just above the horizon line and rotates around us, casting a long shadow off the contours of the mountain that rises ahead of us.

Touch

There is nothing here to touch. That's for the best. With temperatures of forty below zero, any exposed skin would freeze in seconds. And so I am encased in a high-tech armor, further disconnecting me from an environment that offers nothing more than wind, cold, and the challenge of scaling an ice-encrusted mountain.

All climbers assemble their own suit of armor, and I'm benefiting from the most advanced threads that science has to offer.

My protection against the forty-below temperature starts with a base layer of polypropylene. The fibers of the material are thin yet more absorbent than a kitchen sponge. If you put a drop of water on it, you'll see the water spread out as wide as a pancake. By spreading out, the material allows your body heat to evaporate the water quickly. Even if you sweat like a horse, polypro can keep you dry to the touch.

Cotton, by contrast, is the devil's fabric. It takes longer to dry, draws more heat out of the body, and leaves you cold and wet. When I'm on an expedition, my cotton T-shirts stay clean and folded, in a drawer back at home where they belong.

The next layer, over the polypro, provides insulation against the subzero temperatures and takes a couple different forms: fleece or down. Fleece traps anywhere from 30 percent to about 80 percent of your body heat. So you wear it when you're active to vent some of your heat to ensure that you don't get too hot. Overheating would sap your strength, like sitting in a sauna.

If you're inactive, loafing in a tent, then you need to retain more of your body heat to stay warm. In that case, a puffy down jacket is the ideal choice with the down feathers trapping air and retaining up to 95 percent of your body heat. But there is a risk to down. If it gets wet, it loses all ability to keep you warm. The feathers clump, soaking up the water, and the insulating air layer vanishes, dissipating the heat and leaving you fully exposed to the cold and wind.

The insulating layer for my feet gets special attention. My toes have been highly susceptible to frostbite ever since I spent twenty-four hours in the death zone on Everest. My boots have a thick layer of closed-cell foam, similar in concept to the material used on the tiles of the Space Shuttle to insulate its fuselage against the temperature swings of reentry.

My final layer is a shell that armors me against the eighty-mile-an-hour wind gusts and waterproofs me from the swirling snow. A lightweight, completely waterproof, and breathable shell requires some high-tech trickery. The critical, enabling scientific fact is that a drop of water is vastly larger than a molecule of water vapor—a basketball compared to a BB. So a material, say Gore-Tex, has pores small enough that they allow vapor, excess body heat, to escape while keeping large water droplets from getting in. In fact, the pores in a waterproof shell are typically twenty thousand times smaller than a raindrop of water but one thousand times bigger than a water vapor molecule.

All that gear is jammed into my sled, a runnerless toboggan, sealed shut with ropes and bungee cord. The toboggan has a harness attached, the sort of thing that an Antarctic explorer in the 1900s would have slung onto a workhorse or sled dog. We have neither of those. We're the pack animals.

Jim and I each clip a harness around our waist and begin pulling our loads up the mountain.

I confess, I'm a lousy sled dog; I don't get a thrill out of hauling gear.

I would never qualify to be a lead husky, that snarling dog with harness taut, eager for the day's haul. I would take my place in the second row, or third, reluctant to be hooked on to the line, looking longingly at the sledge, wondering why I couldn't ride on it instead. And that night, after gnawing our meals down to the bone, while the other dogs dreamed of the next day's haul, their legs jerking in running motions, I would dream of a paw massage.

At least a real sled dog would end the day's haul with a slab of meat. Mine ends with Cup-a-Soup and a bag of dehydrated stroganoff.

For the next five days, we have astounding luck: we get day after day of clear weather. It is windy and relentlessly cold, reaching only twenty below at the warmest, but no snow falls that would pin us in place. We climb uninterrupted, making camps to rest along the way to the summit.

Our first camp sits on an exposed open expanse of ice. As we unclip from our harnesses, the wind is beating on us, swirling and whipping around, lashing at our backs and gear. A tent can't withstand these stinging gusts. So we pull saws and shovels off our sleds and start carving blocks out of the ice beneath our feet.

We slice out ice block after ice block, each about the size of a breadbox, and stack them to make a four-foot-high protective horseshoe of ice that rims our tent. The wind can now blow as hard as it wants—it can bend its head and bull-rush our camp—and our tent, cushioned by the wall, will stand strong.

The masonry work leaves us drained, and we crawl into the tent and start unloading food. One thing we don't have to haul with us is water. We're surrounded by it; 70 percent of all of the earth's freshwater is locked up in the ice of Antarctica. With a snap of a lighter and the burst of flame from a camp stove we can melt all the water we need.

Camp stoves are temperamental things. Despite careful cleaning, they still sputter, choke, and wheeze. They have these bouts of asthma at the worst possible times. If you have a comfortable rest day in the tent, the stove lights promptly, pushing out a stout blue flame. But every so often, when you are cold and depleted, energy draining away, your body desperate for water and food, the stove seizes up, gasps, and lies quiet.

On this occasion, the stove lights promptly, reserving its seizure for a more desperate hour.

We've picked this time to bed down because the sun, perpetually rotating around us just above the horizon line, is about to disappear behind the mountain, taking the temperature down with it. Since time is meaningless here, we decided that when the mountain blots out the sun, we'll call it 10 P.M. I drop my head down on a sack stuffed with clothes and gear and wake hours later to a light-filled tent. Two days later I'll stand on the summit.

I wish I could say that the view from the summit was captivating in the clear Antarctic skies. But to me, it wasn't compelling. Unlike other mountaintops I've stood on, there were no sharp ridgelines or granite faces to hold the eye, no green valley in the distance or glacier contoured like the raked sand of a golf trap. We stared out over an endless sheet of crumpled white paper. It was another summit; another place to turn around. Box checked.

Other people could find beauty in that view, I'm sure. I lived in rural Illinois for nearly seven years and I know that there are farmers who can look out over the miles of uninterrupted stalks and be filled with a sense of wonder, overcome by nature's splendor. I just see corn.

The good weather continued on our descent and the Otter picked us up, as planned, five days after dropping us off. Despite being in the most remote and unforgiving place on the planet, it seemed that our good luck was holding and that we would get out of Antarctica and back home quicker than any other climb I had done before.

But our luck was about to change.

There are storms, and then there are wrathful, unforgiving tempests, with the fury to bend steel and the determination to unearth your deepest fears. If there is a measure to the severity of these tempests, it can be revealed by the Hercules cargo plane. The Herc is designed to land in any conditions the world can hurl at it, having the tenacity and slow steady power to punch through the teeth of a storm, land, and haul away a load.

When the Otter landed us back at the depot, we got the news. The Herc crew canceled their supply flight due to an incoming storm. That could mean only one thing: the approaching blizzard would be impenetrable.

Every generation has its memorable competitors: Magic vs. Bird, Ali vs. Frazier, Sea Biscuit vs. War Admiral. In 1911, it was Robert Scott vs. Roald Amundsen to see who would be the first to reach the South Pole. Both were trying to bring the prestige home for their respective countries, Scott for England and Amundsen for Norway.

There was talk of scientific work along the way—mapping, cataloguing, and measurements—but for Scott the expedition had only one true purpose: to secure the Pole for the British Empire. He had failed in his previous expeditions, but he was determined to reach the Pole this time.

Scott's confidence was admirable, but entirely misplaced. There is little one can be sure of when trying to survive on the vast Antarctic ice sheet. It was a trip that would take months, covering more than one thousand miles across the harshest and most desolate terrain in the world. There would be no possibility for rescue should something go wrong, no exit strategy. Scott's confidence couldn't warm the hands in a subzero chill; it couldn't calm the winds or put food in an empty tin. It was logistics, not ego, that his team needed most.

Scott planned to reach the Pole by establishing camps along the way to support slow but steady progress. This was the same technique later used in the first summits of Everest and El Capitan.

The expedition would be spread over two seasons: the first to establish supply caches, the second to use those caches to push on to the Pole and back.

Effective caching required the placement of tons of supplies and would be an expedition in itself, involving a team of dozens of men, dog sleds, and horses. The location of the caches was critical and carefully planned. Pushing the tons of supplies forward one mile at a time was an enormous effort, so the caches would be placed not one inch further along than necessary.

The key camp, the camp their lives would depend on, they nicknamed One Ton Depot. This massive cache of supplies had to be placed at just the right spot so that it could support the expedition the next season both on its way toward the Pole and on return when they would be dangerously depleted. The position of eighty degrees south latitude was calculated to be the ideal location. In hindsight, it is remarkable how prescient the determination of that very spot turned out to be.

As the team pushed on toward eighty degrees south latitude to establish the cache, storms lashed at them and delayed progress, horses fell ill, the Antarctic winter approached, and Scott began considering whether to establish One Ton Depot thirty-five miles north of the planned location. That would mean that the next season, as they were returning from the South Pole hungry and worn, the camp would be thirty-five miles further away than originally planned.

Scott was strongly advised to keep pushing on and not establish One Ton short of the strategically calculated location. Otherwise, his assistant Lawrence Oates warned, "I'm afraid you'll come to regret not taking my advice."

There are always a few preplanned decisions that can be revisited when circumstances get difficult. You may decide to leave the coffee grinder behind, or determine that the pillow really isn't critical. In contrast, there are decisions that should never be revisited because they were so carefully considered in the first place. The location of his most critical food cache at eighty degrees south latitude in Antarctica was one of those decisions that Scott should never have reconsidered. But he did.

Scott decided to establish One Ton Depot at seventy-nine degrees, twenty-nine minutes south latitude, thirty-five miles short of the original plan. That decision would be his team's undoing.

On the 13th of September, 1911, after living through months of total darkness, and with the worst of the Antarctic winter behind them, Scott and his team began their march toward the Pole.

As they pushed forward, Scott made another fateful decision. While they had originally planned for four members to be on the final push, he raised the number to five. There would now be one more mouth to feed. But with weather cooperating and food evidently plentiful, Scott estimated they would have no problems bringing the extra man along. Optimistic, they pressed on.

On January 17, 1912, Scott's team finally approached the South Pole.

The expedition had left Wales eighteen months earlier, camping through the harsh Antarctic winter. Scott had personally suffered through previous failed expeditions; he had witnessed scurvy and storms, confronted fears and desperation, had seen team members die. Perhaps he rationalized it would all be worth it now. The misery that he had endured, all the families that were left alone and fatherless by his expeditions, could now be balanced by, perhaps even justified by, this moment, when his boot finally touched the South Pole.

What he saw next must have crushed him.

As his team neared the Pole, there, in front of him, was Roald Amundsen's flag, planted thirty-two days earlier.

If the team had been first, maybe it would have buoyed their spirits, provided a bit more will to persevere through what was to come. Being second, spirits sank. Scott wrote these words in his diary:

Great God! This is an awful place and terrible enough for us to have laboured to it without the reward of priority.

And with that, he turned his men toward home.

The diary reveals that on the return trip, despite the rapidly deteriorating condition of his team, Scott had them load thirty pounds of rock samples onto their sleds. Perhaps to counter the overwhelming sense of defeat, he could motivate his team by some appeal to scientific purpose. As a physicist I'm enthused and motivated by science, but I'll admit that under those circumstances, having suffered such defeat, a rock would have provided me no consolation at all.

By mid-February, they had not yet arrived at One Ton Depot, that critical supply camp they had established a season earlier. A blizzard was now setting in and it was clear that they did not have enough food for all of them to last out a long storm.

Heroism can take various forms. It can be brazen, or shrill, or thoughtful. In the case of one of the team members, Lawrence Oates, the very man who had warned about the placement of One Ton Depot, his heroism came in the form of modest resignation. According to Scott's diary, on March 17, Oates made an announcement to the team:

"I am just going outside and I may be some time."

Oates then walked out into the blizzard and, by his own choice, froze to death. With that decision, he left one fewer mouth to feed and perhaps, he hoped, that would provide a better chance for the others to survive.

Oates's act of heroism merely prolonged the inevitable. On March 29, with the storm still raging, Scott began the final entry in his diary, discovered eight months later along with his body and those of his teammates.

Last entry. For Gods sake look after our people.

That final entry was accompanied by a private letter to his wife and another letter to the British public, which closed with these words:

Had we lived, I should have had a tale to tell of the hardihood, endurance, and courage of my companions which would have stirred the heart of every Englishman. These rough notes and our dead bodies must tell the tale, but surely, surely, a great rich country like ours will see that those who are dependent on us are properly provided for.

Scholars have been studying Scott's expedition for nearly a century, debating whether his decisions deserve praise or vilification, whether he demonstrated leadership or ineptitude. I have no strong opinion on those matters.

Instead, what I find compelling is how he spent those final hours with the pen, coming to grips with his death, the deprivation of Antarctica now fully realized. All three of his final writings—his diary, his letter to his wife, and his letter to the public—end with a common focus: a reflection on his family. Yet they were more than ten thousand miles away, too distant to hear his final desperate whispers.

He and his remaining expedition mates died an Antarctic death: isolated, disconnected, and desolate, their bodies frozen into place, their spirits shattered into pieces.

Scott died, they all died, *cold and broken*.

For what it's worth, they were just eleven miles away from One Ton Depot, the cache that had all the food and supplies they needed to survive. The opportunity to live was there, so close, yet they couldn't reach it.

With the Hercules grounded, we braced for the incoming storm.

We surrounded our tents with ice walls that could withstand winds of more than one hundred miles per hour. We had plenty of food and I had a few books to read. The storm, no matter its fury, would be manageable. We could wait it out.

The blizzard hit a few hours later, battering us as we retreated to tents.

During a break in the blizzard we strapped on cross-country skis and glided over the ice sheet with our Global Positioning System firmly in hand. Without a GPS, it would be nearly impossible, merely a matter of luck, to find our way back to camp. Within a few hundred yards of skiing out, our camp vanished in the swirling snowdrift. Once the bright yellow of our tents faded from view, the landscape looked the same in all directions, completely flat, the horizon line blending in with the clouds.

There was nothing to see, no contour to the surface, it was like being on a treadmill in a fogbank. Still, the skiing, as dull as it was, passed some time before the blizzard picked up again and we returned to our tents. I zipped shut the flap and returned to a book and the thick down of my sleeping bag.

That is how time passed for me, hour after hour, day after day. Eventually, I ran out of books. I lay there, zipped up in a bag, confined, staring at the tent walls just inches away.

Detached. Isolated. Waiting out the storm; the days wore on. The solitude bore down on me.

I was thirty-eight years old and experiencing pure detachment from the world—a detachment that I had thought, until now, I had desired.

I was alone with my thoughts. I began to reflect on why people might conclude that I was cold and broken. I thought about whether I wanted to stay that way.

My father, an English professor, was probably the first adult to see my emotions chill and crack. After my mother died he was left to raise three teenage boys on his own in the suburbs of Virginia.

Not unexpectedly, as we got older, we all went our different ways.

My middle brother, Joe, who is two years older than me, is now a surgeon in the navy, having been deployed to hospitals all across the globe over the years as medical help was needed. His last decade of deployments reads like a list of political hot spots: he served in Iraq, standing in the blood of fallen soldiers, went to Guantánamo Bay to treat detainees, provided emergency surgeries after Hurricane Katrina and the earthquake in Haiti.

My oldest brother, Roger, who is five years older than me, lives in the Midwest. He started out as a mechanic and eventually became a manager for an airline company, moving several times over the last ten years to accommodate the changes to an industry that was shaken after 9/11 and continues to expand and contract.

There aren't many occasions when we are all at the same place at the same time. The only time when we were around the table together with any regularity was more than three decades ago. One of those times none of us has ever forgotten.

Despite the challenges of raising us, my father was determined to keep our minds clear and our backs strong. To do that, he relied on what had shaped him.

My father was raised during the Great Depression, which means that he sweeps his spatula around the glass of the mustard jar and holds it up to the light to look for any last smears of yellow. By the time he's done, the jar glistens as if it were buffed clear by a machinist.

His Depression experience also means that we didn't click on the air conditioner in the summer unless the temperature was over ninety-five degrees. We wore thick sweaters in the winter. We hand-washed the dishes. We had a manual push lawnmower.

It was so rare that we watched TV or went out to the movies that I grew up without any awareness of pop culture. It wasn't until I was in graduate school, when a girlfriend bought me a television, that the world started to penetrate. She had delivered it to me with the following order: "Watch this. You're clueless." I first saw *Star Wars* when a buddy rented the video and showed it at his house. That was in 1994, nearly twenty years after the movie came out. When I did finally see an episode of *Seinfeld,* it was the finale and I didn't get any of the jokes.

What really marked our days growing up, more than anything else, was the food that my dad would put on the table. We didn't eat lettuce; we ate kale. He didn't use wheat flour; he used bulgur. We didn't have chocolate; we had carob. We drank powdered milk. I assumed as I was growing up that these substitutions were a result of his suffering through the Great Depression, when, I imagined, he ate cardboard with a side dish of shoe leather.

He kept the desserts ordinary at least. Except once.

I can't remember who asked first, that night around the dinner table when I was thirteen years old, but it was on all our minds.

"What is this?"

We had dutifully plowed through our dinner, forking into our mouths whatever bizarre vegetable my father had purchased that week. Now dessert was in front of us, but it was unidentifiable.

The bowl was filled with a thick pale yellow sludge. Trapped in the paste were small pods, like maggots with glistening translucent shells. At least nothing appeared to be moving in the bowl, which was encouraging.

"It's rice pudding," my dad calmly explained. He had been answering this question for years, just never over dessert.

I tapped at it with my spoon, examining the texture. I pried out one of the maggots.

"This is rice?"

"Yes."

"Then why make dessert out of it?"

To this day, I still think that is a sensible question. After all, no one eats string bean cake or cauliflower cookies.

"Because it tastes good," my father responded.

Perhaps in some cultures, on some tables, in someone else's kitchen, that might be true. But that day, licking a smear of it off my spoon, I can tell you with certainty that it wasn't good.

"No thanks," I said. The Slakey brothers all looked at one another and we leaned back from our bowls, spoons idle on the table.

My father decided at that moment that he had to seize control. "This isn't an option; you're eating that rice pudding."

We had squared off over dinners before, eventually complying with an order to eat some mossy green or other. But this time, I thought, justice was on our side. No one is required to eat dessert. In fact, dessert is supposed to be the reward for slogging through the main course. This was like telling the winner of the Boston Marathon that his reward is that he now gets to walk home. In the rain. Barefoot. Over glass.

It didn't come to blows, it never did in our house. My father had earned our respect; we all recognized the challenge he faced raising us all alone, so a smack was never necessary.

And so, knowing we would never get physically harmed, we decided to wait him out, in silence, ignoring the pudding and thinking that at some point he would concede because no one can, truly, force you to eat dessert.

He had an appointment that night so he walked out of the kitchen a few minutes later, leaving the three of us brothers still sitting at the table with our full untouched dessert bowls. When he pulled the door shut behind him, we took our bowls over to the sink and dumped the contents down the drain. We left the kitchen feeling victorious.

It's very rare now, but occasionally we find ourselves all together around a table, and one of us will make a joke about that ridiculous pudding situation and we'll all laugh. And on one of those occasions I asked my dad what he was thinking that night when he tried to force us to eat that pudding. He shrugged off the question.

So, many years later, I'm left to imagine the answer on my own. When he returned home that night and looked in the sink, he would have seen the discarded pile of rice; we didn't make any attempt to hide it. He would have taken that spatula and scraped the final remains down the sink, the effort to make a treat for us ending in nothing but failure. He always projected steel, but at that moment, alone, watching the grains spiral down the drain, I imagine he thought about our mom and how different all this would be if she were standing there beside him.

She was no longer standing beside me, or my brothers either. As a result, all of us retreated, each in our own way. None of us had many close friends. There were many evenings as an adult when I would be at home, alone, doing little more than sitting under the lamplight.

And now I was alone again, in my tent, waiting out a blizzard in Antarctica. Over the next eight days, I recognized that my life was like Scott's death—isolated, cold, broken. I realized that this was no way for me to live. Or, to be more honest, I knew that it was not the way I wanted to die. If I kept going the way I was, my final moments would be every bit as miserable as Scott's.

We could hear the Herc before we could see it. The sound filled the clearing sky and then the flying walrus appeared on the horizon. After eight days, the blizzard had finally broken.

I was relieved to leave the continent.

The sensory deprivation tank of Antarctica had presented me with isolation in its purest form. The hour upon hour, zipped up, alone, in the tent had given me a chance to consider, to feel, the consequences of pure detachment. I had thought about what isolation had made of me and what it had done to Robert Falcon Scott.

Until this expedition, I had thought I was entirely comfortable with distance and detachment. But I had never before experienced them with such intensity, the total separation, that Antarctica presented.

I had thought it was my remove and self-absorption that gave me the focus to push past challenges and achieve my goals. But there was Robert Scott to consider. Those qualities had delivered him a death in silence and despair.

So I had an epiphany of sorts. I decided that I had enough. It was time I left my cave.

It was a quiet epiphany. I heard no voice. Clouds didn't part. Instead, I came to my realization after days of being confined in a tent, thinking about my mother and the past, feeling the desolation of

Antarctica in the present, and reliving so much that had happened in between.

I remember worrying about one thing: I still had a half dozen more items on my surfing and climbing To Do List. As I thawed, would I risk going soft and losing what I thought was the necessary steel in the spine to get it all done?

When I returned home from Antarctica I committed to a couple of things. From here on out, I would do what I could to make every expedition more pleasurable. I would participate in the camaraderie.

The next thing I did was pick up the phone and call Gina Eppolito.

Gina's mother, I later learned, was born in Paganica, Italy. Gina's father was Sicilian. And Gina was born in Brooklyn, New York. So she was a first-generation Brooklyn Italian. This meant two things.

First, despite being only five foot four and standing lower than a lunch counter, Gina could still shoulder her way up to the front of the line, shout out her order, and walk out of the deli with her sandwich ahead of all those guys who towered over her.

Second, she could squeeze seventy-two minutes of activity into every hour.

Along with those two qualities came a tenderness and generosity and, of course, a desire for adventure, which is what took her to Everest in the first place.

And there were a few more things, completely unexpected, highly unlikely similarities between her life and mine. Like me, Gina was the youngest of three siblings—her two sisters were nearly the same ages as my two brothers. She too had suffered through the loss of a close family member to cancer. She was raised by a single parent, a determined mother whose firm spine, like my father's, was forged by the Great Depression.

I would discover, eventually, that it wasn't these similarities that would draw us together; it would be the differences. But for now, and for one of the first times in my life, I started a relationship that was more than just a way to fill my evenings.

I asked her years later why she agreed to go out with me, after I had made those insulting comments about her photography while we were on Everest. She replied in a way that was so consistent with her character.

Gina was a marathoner; on one of her training runs for Boston she ran twenty miles in a cold sleet, coming home dripping and numb. And so she saw something interesting about me, despite the thick exterior. She had stood at Everest Base Camp and seen the snow blowing furiously off the summit, thrown a half mile out into the sky. The drive that got me there appealed to her.

But that wasn't all. She confessed that there was one more thing that led to her seeing me again. It was something that would be a lasting difference between us. It was her notion of fate.

Gina was in the darkroom with a friend the day she developed the picture she took of our climbing team at Base Camp. She had dropped the photo paper into the basin of chemicals and in the dim red light she watched the images begin to emerge. The climbers started taking shape, details of faces, gear, the tent slowly coming into focus on the thin white sheet.

She pulled the paper out of the chemical solution and held it up for a closer look. Her friend leaned in and asked about the people in the picture.

There in the bottom right corner was the climber who had made the comments about her pet photography. Without knowing why, but with complete certainty, she pointed at me.

"I have a feeling I'll know him for a very long time."

———

The next summer, in 2001, I traveled to Alaska with Tom Paxton to climb the highest peak in North America.

The peak, Denali, is a native Alaskan word meaning Great One. It's a boastful name, but entirely appropriate since it does in fact have a massive vertical rise, higher than Everest. Everest peaks at 29,029 feet, the highest point on the planet, but its base sits on the Tibetan Plateau at roughly 17,000 feet, giving it a total vertical rise of roughly 12,000 feet. The base of Denali, by contrast, sits at 2,000 feet, giving its mammoth block of granite a total rise of 18,320 feet.

There are a variety of routes to the top of Denali. Some are isolated, require careful planning, precision, and leave one exposed to the elements. There are other routes, like the West Buttress, that are easier, populated by other climbers, and a more social scene. A year earlier, before my Antarctica experience, my pick of route would have been different, but now I chose the West Buttress.

One of the first climbers that Pax and I met on the route was Mike McCabe. He was wearing a pair of worn college gym shorts, grinning, bare-legged in the cold bite of a breezy ten-degree day. An energetic scrappy Coloradan, he had recently sold his company, MakeTheMove .com, and was now spending his days in the mountains.

According to Mike, his company had managed to survive the dot-com collapse of April 2000 for a good reason. Most of the dot-coms back in 2000 were speculative, thin concepts hoping to explode into an actual product. By contrast, he actually had a business plan; he provided a genuine service. If you were planning to move, you could go onto the site, type in your old address and your new address, and with a push of a button it would cancel your newspaper, phone service, and utilities, and restart them in your new location.

I appreciated Mike's business plan; I could relate. I had moved fourteen times over the previous twenty years. Sometimes I would move to a different state, other times across town. One time I moved forty feet down the hall just to get an apartment that had a bit more light.

But all that was in the past, and on this expedition I was about to learn the value of community.

A climber doesn't spend much time actually scaling the West Buttress of Denali. Most of the time is spent hauling freight up and down the mountain performing the familiar routine of establishing camps and supply caches.

One of the biggest one-day pushes on the route requires hauling a load of supplies about three thousand feet up the mountain. The sky was thick with clouds the morning we had planned to make that push. We knew it would storm, but if we waited for the weather to blow over we could lose three days and be behind schedule. The day's haul wasn't a technically demanding section of the climb, and so without any discussion we pushed on.

Climbing has its glorious moments where the strain and labor of the day are rewarded with a sense of tremendous physical achievement or a spectacular vista. This was not one of those times.

The next few hours were tiresome, we were little more than pack animals, trudging mindlessly up the mountain. By the time we had ascended two thousand feet, the snow was coming down hard. The weather wasn't worrisome; all of us had climbed through far worse storms. Still, the storm was annoying, requiring more and more effort to punch through the accumulating snow.

As the day wore on we found less to talk about, heads down, feet driving forward, all of us focused on getting the pile of supplies up to the next camp. I started thinking about the fifty pounds of gear that I was dragging up on the sled behind me, scrolling through the items one by one in my mind. Why did we bring the coffee press? Those refinements are fine at a low camp where the Twin Otter had dropped us off, but why drag it up here? And did I really need the down footwarmers? I had imagined casually sipping freshly ground coffee, enjoying the cold night air, feet in the down warmers resting on top of my pack.

I had gone from being a stripped-down-to-the-basics climber, to loading my duffel bag with luxury items that could transform a desolate camp into a Four Seasons experience. My determination post-Antarctica to keep these climbs entertaining had gotten the better of me, starting with the French roast.

When we finally arrived at the cache site, the snow was falling hard, visibility had dropped to a dozen feet. It was late afternoon, hours later than we had expected it would take to get to this point, and we still had to dig a four-foot-deep hole in the snow to bury and secure our supplies.

Mike, Pax, and I dropped our packs and stared down at the snow. No one spoke; the minutes ticked by.

It had to be done, we had to spend the next half hour in mindless digging, an inglorious mountaineering moment. We picked up our shovels and slammed them into the snow.

I was annoyed, pure and simple. The day had deteriorated into the common drudgery of hauling and digging.

I tossed a load of snow over my shoulder and drove the shovel back into the hole.

Another load over the shoulder, another plunge back into the hole.

How could anyone ever enjoy doing this?

Toss. Plunge.

I'm pissed off at this hole.

Toss. Plunge.

"Bring it, Slake."

Evidently, I had been saying those thoughts out loud, and Pax was now joining in.

"Get angry, amigos. Channel it. We can use it."

Toss. Plunge. We were all in a rhythm now.

My mom, Zaida Sojos-Vela, in the early 1950s, before she left Ecuador for the United States. She died when I was eleven. "Be strong" was her final message to me, but it took me thirty-five years to understand what that meant.

The Slakey boys. Rog (standing on Dad's right) and Joe (on Dad's left) say it was my competition with them that made me want to climb and surf the world.

On the way up Mount Everest, our climbing team visited the remote monastery of Thyangboche to receive a good-luck blessing from the Most Holy Rinpoche. This was where my climbing and surfing journey took its first unexpected turn.

Every pile of stones in this remote plain is a memorial to a fallen climber and a reminder that the decisions made on mountains are significant and irreversible. Do I push through the storm or turn home? Facing those decisions is why I climb. *Photo by Mike Farris*

LEFT: The Rinpoche gave me this amulet, etched with letters that the Sherpas said conveyed "life's meaning." I would neglect it for years before becoming determined to decode its message. *Photo by Matthew Girard*

BELOW: Jim Williams (*foreground*) and me at an Everest Base Camp blessing. The other climbers were attentive, but I tuned out, entirely disinterested in the spiritual ceremonies.

I'm peeling off gear after summiting Everest in a blizzard in 2000. Just below the summit I encountered a Sherpa who had decided to sit down in the snow and die. His decision didn't square with my worldview: push on and climb to the last breath.

Our team is dug in, awaiting an oncoming blizzard in Antarctica. The sensory deprivation of that wasteland led me to consider why so many people found me cold and detached. *Photo by Jim Williams*

After a quiet epiphany in Antarctica, I took a more leisurely approach to my next climb, the West Buttress of Denali, where beach umbrellas populate one of the high camps. *Photo by Mike Farris*

Relaxing with Gina after a day of surfing in Bali, Indonesia. Within hours I would pick up a local paper and read about the ambush of Americans on a road through the Freeport-McMoRan mine. I had dodged a bullet: I had been on that road days earlier, traveling through the mine under cover of night to climb Puncak Jaya.

Our mutt, Pemba, is named after the Sherpa word for Saturday, the day I got her from the shelter. She cleaned up nicely; eventually, I did too. The dog was a turning point with Gina. *Photo by Gina Eppolito*

Gina and I return to the Thyangboche monastery for our wedding day.

BELOW: Our twin girls, Kinley (*left*), the Lama's namesake, and Zaida (*right*), my mother's namesake. *Photo by Gina Eppolito*

Dump trucks would spend months filling in a gulley and rerouting a road to keep from angering the Snake Goddess of Bhutan. It was one of a string of events that challenged my scientific views. *Photo by Gina Eppolito*

Gina and I, standing beside Kinle, the Lama of Dhorika, who invited us to visit his remote village in Bhutan.

Staring out over the rooftops of old Delhi, I finally saw the richness of the world. *Photo by Gina Eppolito*

I finished my twelve-year-long journey on Vestvågøy Island in Norway. I surfed the Arctic Ocean and discovered the meaning of the amulet. *Photo by Cody Duncan*

Toss. Plunge. All angry. All digging ferociously. All with a shared purpose.

In just minutes we had dug down four feet. Within another fifteen minutes the supplies were in, the snow piled back up, a marker in place. That was one of the most productive bouts of anger I have ever had.

And it was clear, at that moment, standing over a hole that my friends and I had dug in record time, that I was better off with them than without them.

We arrived back in camp a couple of hours later, moving quickly, having lightened our load by the nearly two hundred pounds we had deposited in the hole. As I approached my tent, I realized something was missing. Before leaving that morning I had sunk my ice axe into the snow, right by the front flap of the tent. Now it was gone.

I had an attachment to that axe; it had been with me for every mountain I had ever climbed. It was one of the most dependable pieces of climbing equipment I owned.

There were a dozen other climbers at the camp and I asked around to see if anyone saw who grabbed it. I got no leads, but I did get a common response: "Drag. You're going to need that to summit."

Indeed I would. There are a couple of steep sections to the climb and the ice axe is a key safety device. The axe allows for self-rescue in the event of a fall. A climber sliding down the mountainside can slam the teeth of the axe into the snow as a brake. Without it, the slide continues unabated to its inevitable conclusion, depositing the climber in a broken pile at the bottom of the mountain.

Whoever took my axe knew that. They knew that they were pulling out of my hands a critical piece of safety equipment. They would know it would be too risky for me to continue up without it. When they pulled my axe out of its parking place near my tent that morning, they killed my chance to summit.

Then I started to have doubts.

This could never have happened in Antarctica, because only our team was on the mountain so there wouldn't have been any outsiders thieving gear. And if I hadn't picked this social route on Denali, and had instead followed the solitary path, this would never have happened. It seemed that being disconnected, detached from other climbers, provided a certain measure of security and control.

My new, more social approach to climbing was being put to an immediate test.

I don't remember the name of the climber who walked by me at that moment, heading down the mountain. I should remember, after all: two weeks later I would be filling out his name and address on a FedEx package.

"Hey, man. What's up?"

"Someone stole my ice axe. No one at camp knows who took it."

"Drag. You're going to need that to summit."

Another fruitless conversation.

"You know what, dude? Take mine. I'm on my way down the mountain. I'm done with it."

It says something about me that it never occurred to me to ask a descending climber if I could borrow an axe. It seems so obvious now, but it didn't then. In fact, I might have turned and gone back down the mountain if it wasn't for that climber, thoughtful and generous, holding out his ice axe, offering it to me.

"Got a pen?" he asked.

I wrote down his address and promised to ship it back to him the moment I got back home.

"I hope you have more luck with it than I did. I didn't summit."

We shook hands and he continued on down the mountain. The next day I continued up.

A few days later Mike, Pax, and I were standing on the summit of Denali. It was nearly cloudless, only a light breeze blowing, a comfortable ten degrees in the sun. An animated world stretched out past our feet, down the crags of snow-covered granite, across a radiant glacier, and on into the lush forest that filled the valley floor a dozen miles away. There was a full palette of colors, all visible, all vibrant.

We turned and followed our tracks back down the ridgeline to camp, fulfilled.

It was the goodwill of that climber—his sense of shared purpose, his desire to assist in someone else's time of need—who made that summit possible and allowed me to tick item number 6 off the To Do List.

I would soon develop my own sense of shared purpose. In a few months' time, I would dodge a bullet that would hit someone else in the back and forever change her life and mine.

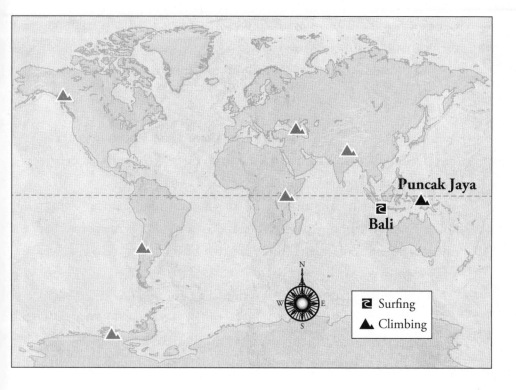

Puncak Jaya

Bali

Surfing
Climbing

Chapter 6

THE AMBUSH

———

Bullets from a Steyr assault rifle can tear through the side of a jeep as if the doors are made of paper. They cross the next few inches to the passenger in fractions of a second. As the lead contacts the human body, its heat vaporizes the skin, then burrows forward, splintering on the bone, breaking into a hundred pieces that penetrate the organs and then cool into hard blackened flakes.

I would come to understand all this in the jungles of Indonesia.

By the summer of 2002, I had only one mountain left on my surfing and climbing To Do List. But I hit a snag: there is contentious debate over where that last high point is.

I had stood on the summit of the highest mountain in Africa, South America, Europe, Asia, Antarctica, and North America. What was the seventh continent? There are two possible answers: Australia and Oceania.

If the correct answer is Australia, then the highest peak I had left to climb was Mount Kosciuszko, which stands at 7,310 feet. If Oceania is the answer, then I would climb Puncak Jaya in the jungles of West Papua, New Guinea, Indonesia, with an elevation of 16,024 feet.

Which is it? Since my surfing and climbing record was dependent on the correct choice, I decided to do some research.

The Seven Summits had become a well-established activity by this time. A few devotees maintain diligent records of the people who succeed, carefully documenting the dates and peaks. I consulted the list and found that previous climbers were no more certain than I was about the definition of the seventh continent. Three lists are maintained: climbers who summit the peak in Indonesia, climbers who summit the peak in Australia, and climbers who are so uncertain that they summit both just to be sure. Since those lists didn't settle the matter, I searched other sources.

Here is what you will find if you look up "continent" in the Merriam-Webster online dictionary:

con•ti•nent

Pronunciation: \\'kän-tə-nənt, 'känt-nənt

Function: *noun*

1 *archaic* : container, confines

2 *archaic* : epitome

3 : mainland

4 : one of the six or seven great divisions of land on the globe

Look hard at definition #4. "Six or seven"? This is not the kind of authoritative clarification I expected from a dictionary. If I looked up "penny" would they say "a piece of copper with one or two sides"?

With the dictionary waffling, the next natural online resource to check was Wikipedia.

In Wikipedia you will at least learn that there is a vast area of the earth called Oceania, although, they explain, "the boundaries are defined in a number of ways."

"In a number of ways"? That's no help.

I could think of only one way to settle this.

At one time in my life there was a source of information that I never had reason to doubt. It was always reliable and eternally authoritative. I unquestioningly accepted whatever a teacher neatly spelled out on the wide expanse of an elementary school chalkboard. So to settle the matter of whether the seventh continent is Australia or Oceania, I consulted a sixth-grade geography lesson plan.

As it turns out, in sixth grade, or thereabouts, we were taught that the seventh continent is in fact "Oceania." For example, from one lesson planner:

OCEANIA, the smallest continent, is one of the most diverse and fascinating areas on the planet. Collectively it combines all of Australia, New Zealand, Papua New Guinea, as well as the

thousands of coral atolls and volcanic islands of the South Pacific
Ocean, including the Melanesia and Polynesia groups and Micro-
nesia, a widely scattered group of islands that run along the north-
ern and southern edges of the Equator.

That settled the matter: the seventh continent is Oceania, not Australia. I would climb Puncak Jaya, not Kosciuszko.

I'll admit, Puncak Jaya was the mountain I had wanted to climb in the first place because Kosciuszko seemed so unfulfilling. That peak in Australia got its name from the first European to lay eyes on it, Count Paul Edmund Strzelecki, who gave it the name because he thought it resembled the Kosciuszko Mound in his native Poland.

After years of scaling cloud-splitting peaks I did not want to complete the list by climbing something that got its name from a mound.

With the peak selected, I picked up the phone and called Mike McCabe to see if he would join me in an expedition into the jungles of Indonesia.

"Sure. But how do we get to the mountain?"

"We'll work that out," I said, thinking it would be trivial.

There are drawings on a cave in China, dated to around 400 BC, which show men climbing rocks. This has been interpreted to mean that climbing is an inescapable part of the human experience. I have a slightly different view. I think it means that for the last twenty-five hundred years there have always been men who have had too much free time. And they get into trouble because of it. I certainly did.

Traveling to Indonesia comes with a risk. Since achieving its independence from the Dutch in 1949, Indonesia has been the stage for guerrilla warfare, military assaults, and massacres. Every decade brings another disaster. There were mass killings in the 1960s, thousands killed in a street protest in the 1980s, bloody violence in East Timor throughout the 1990s. And now the U.S. government posts travel warnings highlighting the emergence of terrorist training grounds.

In all my years of traveling, I'd always managed to steer clear of local political trouble. I figured we would go, climb, leave, end of story.

Mike and I came up with a straightforward plan. We would land in the capital city of Jakarta, on the island of Java, and catch a flight to Timika, a small town in the eastern province of Papua. From there, we would hire a helicopter to take us as close as possible to the base of Puncak Jaya.

The helicopter ride was advertised on an Indonesian Web site. The site was in English, catering to precisely what Mike and I had in mind. I swapped e-mails with the company and secured confirmation, as easy as that.

We estimated a seven-day round-trip for the climb. A snap.

In hindsight I should have picked up the phone and made direct contact with the helicopter operators before we left the United States. The site appeared reliable, their e-mails reassuring, but a brief call would have pulled back the curtain and revealed the sketchiness of the operation. With that one call, we might have recognized that they were unreliable, looked for another option, and then the climb—and the next seven years of my life—would have unfolded much differently.

Downtown Jakarta looks as if a collection of modern glass and steel buildings were air-dropped into the middle of a shantytown. The transition from modern to ramshackle, from rich to poor, happens in just a few paces down a block. Within one hundred feet, you can travel through a culinary time tunnel descending from four-star restaurants to smoky street food.

I've always enjoyed sampling a meal scooped onto a plate from the ladle of a street vendor. My hunt for some local food would always start the same way. I would say something like "Well, we didn't come all this way to eat McDonald's" and then dive into a mound of some local cuisine. As a result, my expeditions are inevitably punctuated by 2 A.M. retching, with me moaning in a hotel room or in my sleeping bag, body curled into a comma, waiting for the antibiotics to kick in.

These moments are as unforgettable as witnessing a solar eclipse, and they are always accompanied by a strong memory of the food that took me down. There was the rancid water buffalo I ate in Kathmandu. The stinking shashlik in Ashgabat. That bad fig in Samarkand.

I remember sweeping the last bit of curry up from a street vendor's plate in Delhi. I handed him back the plate and he dunked it in a bucket of water as brown as mud, and then he placed it back on top of the stack for the next customer. That meal sidelined me for days. I vowed to use better judgment.

Our first meal in Jakarta was off the main strip, but in what seemed to be a reliable spot. I was proud of myself; this was indeed showing good judgment. First of all, we were sitting down at one of three tables; we weren't on our feet at a vendor's stand squinting through the billowing smoke trying to get a glimpse of whatever was being blackened in a pan.

Second, they appeared to have a menu. At least, there was a sheet of paper at our table with a list of items on it. Not being able to read Bahasa, I wasn't sure what it said. I suppose it could have been an unpaid plumber's bill the owner carelessly left on the table. Still, that would have suggested a concern for plumbing, which is more than I can say for other establishments we'd been to.

Third, and this was the most impressive, they brought out a large tray stacked with bowls full of all their options. We peered out over the display and pointed at the food we were curious about.

That tray of bowls, which seemed to be a positive feature of the restaurant when we ordered, turned out not to be. We had large servings and couldn't finish the meal. So the cook came to our table with the same vast tray we had picked from. He scooped up our remains and ladled them back into the bowls for the next person to eat. I'm not sure exactly what we ate, although now I knew it was what someone else couldn't finish. Miraculously, I didn't end up retching into a sink that night. It was my first bit of luck on the expedition; it was my only luck, as it turned out.

The next morning we had a weather delay; storms were keeping planes grounded. There would be no flights leaving from Jakarta to Timika, where we would begin our climb. With time to kill, we toured the National History Museum.

The museum tells the history of Indonesia in rows of glass-encased dioramas. It became clear from the miniature replicas that the more than 200 million people on Indonesia's seventeen thousand far-flung islands have little to unite them. In the United States, our differences form a melting pot. In Indonesia, it's a powder keg.

There are dozens of guerrilla movements on the islands. Some fight for control of local resources or political autonomy. Others fight to maintain their ethnic identity. Still others, the Muslim extremists, fight to establish strict Islamic law. And fighting them all is the Indonesian military, with a long record of human rights violations.

In the middle of the jungle on Papua, where we were headed, sits Freeport-McMoRan's Grasberg mine, with an estimated deposit of thousands of tons of gold, making it one of the largest in the world. The 1.25 million–acre colossus starts near Timika and runs northeast right up to the base of Puncak Jaya. A Louisiana financier owned the mine; consequently, according to the local Papuans, the bulk of the profits goes to the United States, creating a source of deep resentment.

After a riot by local residents in 1996, the mine's management increasingly began hiring Indonesian soldiers to protect it and keep trespassers off the property.

Clearly, the mine was a political hot spot. Fortunately, we didn't have to worry about that, since we would be helicoptering over it. It was one more local conflict that I could ignore, as I had numerous times before.

The next day the weather cleared and we flew to Timika, where we met Taufan, the operator of the company that we had booked the helicopter ride with. His first words were not encouraging.

"The helicopter is broken. It will not fly."

I don't know anything about helicopters. But we had reconfirmed with him just a few days earlier and I would guess that it is highly unlikely that in such a short amount of time something so disastrous could occur to a helicopter.

I was doubtful. "What happened?"

"It doesn't work," Taufan said matter-of-factly.

I had expected more detail; now I was even more skeptical.

Mike tried a different approach.

"When will it be fixed?" Perhaps we could simply wait this out for a day or two.

"It cannot be."

We could have continued to ask questions, but the outcome was already clear. We wouldn't be helicoptering to the base of the mountain. There probably never was a helicopter.

"What now?" I asked Mike.

We began exploring options. Since the base of the climb sits at the edge of the Freeport mine, we contacted the mine to check whether they would let us pass through. A manager said no; no non-mine employees were allowed on the property.

We settled on an option that is used the world over to open doors that are otherwise closed. In some countries they refer to the method as a "donation" or "gift." Other countries are more straightforward and call it what it is: a bribe. The local travel company that was supposed to provide the helicopter was very willing to help us grease our way through the mine. That may have been their plan all along.

Taufan contacted someone in authority at the military unit patrolling the mine. He passed along some cash, and a military commander agreed to escort us through personally. After midnight that night, the commander pulled up to our hotel in an army jeep, and we jumped in for the long ride.

It was well after midnight when we entered the mine, yet it was alive with activity. Trucks as tall as two-story houses drove by us, hauling load after load down the road. The mountainside was glowing with spotlights that illuminated deep gashes that were being clawed at by the shovels of immense mechanical excavators.

We saw the machinery for miles and miles as we continued up the mountainside. Unrelenting, operating twenty-four hours a day, this was a determined effort to extract every available ounce of gold the ground had to offer.

We still hadn't reached the end of the mine when the sun started to come up. We couldn't risk being spotted by mineworkers, so we pulled into a military base, and were quietly ushered into a barracks. We withdrew from the daylight, out of sight.

That night, we climbed back into the jeep and continued up the mountainside, the grind and rumble of the mine machinery now familiar, the glow of the activity creating a cityscape.

The sudden transition to darkness came as a shock; everything went black as we entered the mineshaft. The jeep's headlights clicked on and pierced through the thick darkness, the driver confident in the turns, selecting the path that would continue to lead us up the mountain amid an octopus of passageways.

We emerged from the shafts at the top of the mine, where a squad of soldiers occupied a machine gun nest strategically placed at the highest point overlooking a valley below. Equipped with floodlights and coffee, their job was to keep the area clear of trespassers—trespassers such as Mike and me.

The commander hopped out of the jeep and walked up to the soldiers in the nest. Evidently, all this had been prearranged; the soldiers expected our arrival. In fact, this didn't seem like the first time the soldiers had seen climbers. I had the impression that this was a steady moneymaking venture for all those involved.

We clarified our plan with the commander, Taufan translating. In five days, we would meet the commander for the return trip out of the mine. We would emerge from the valley below, stepping into view of the floodlights at 10 P.M. The understanding, of course, was that the soldiers who were in the nest securing the mine wouldn't fire their machine guns when they saw us.

With the return arrangements settled, we trekked down the rubble-strewn slope, the floodlights casting our shadows ahead of us.

A few days later, as we stood on the 16,024-foot limestone peak, a light snow began falling. The flakes provided grounding, familiarity; this was a genuine mountainscape. For the first time, and for the only time during the entire climb, we felt we were in the wilderness instead of walking distance from a gold mine.

Right on schedule, at 10 P.M., precisely five days after we were dropped off, we stood just outside the range of the floodlights, whispering to ourselves in the dark perimeter.

I don't recall Mike or myself being nervous, we weren't concerned that the soldiers would fire down on us from the machine gun nest. Taufan had radioed earlier to confirm when we would arrive, and they had assured us that the guards would let us pass without incident.

We stepped into the light.

There were no rifle cracks, no whistle of bullets. All was going according to plan and I assumed we would be safely out of the mine within a few hours.

We hiked up the rubble slope over the planks and stepped into the soldiers' machine gun nest. It was immediately clear that something had gone wrong.

The commander who had driven us up the mine wasn't there. He had sent someone else to drive us. The replacement didn't have any brass on his uniform, not even a stripe. We no longer had a potent military escort. For the first time, I felt a twinge of concern.

Over the next few hours, we drove on in silence. Then, sometime around 2 A.M. I would guess, as we passed the military camp we had stayed at days earlier, an armed posse suddenly stepped out in front of our vehicle.

Our driver came to a stop as men in military uniforms surrounded our jeep, rifles at the ready. Our driver shouted to the soldiers, and one of them began yelling back. As the soldier continued his shouting, the driver turned back to us to explain the situation in broken English.

Amid the chaos, I caught only a few words, but they were troubling. Our driver was now claiming he only had authority to get us through "the top half of the mine." Apparently, we had passed the halfway point in our descent out of the mine and it sounded like he was telling us that someone else, not him, was in charge of "the bottom half."

Evidently, the person who was in charge of the bottom half of the mine was standing in our headlights, surrounded by a half dozen armed soldiers. He knew at least five words of English:

"Get out of the jeep."

I've thought about that moment many times, particularly in light of what would unfold over the next decade.

For so much of my life I had thrived on dramatic moments of consequential decision making. Years earlier, Pax and I went to the Ruth Glacier in Alaska to climb one of the signature mountains in North America. We were two thirds of the way to the summit when we had to rappel down into a notch.

Pax was seventy feet directly above me, preparing to descend the sheer ice wall. In another minute he would touch down beside me and we'd face an irreversible decision. Should we pull the rope, eliminate all possibility of reversing our steps, and commit ourselves to going to the summit?

Two days earlier, in a grocery store in Talkeetna, Alaska, my biggest decision was whether to get a muffin with my coffee. I opted for blueberry and then Pax and I walked into an airplane hangar full of Twin Otters and asked a pilot if he could take us to the glacier.

The Ruth Glacier sits in the heart of the Alaska Range and is scarred by deep crevasses. Fortunately, there are a few patches of smooth, hard, stable ice just long enough and wide enough to land a plane. With a steady hand, the pilot skied his air taxi onto the ice, dropped us off, and flew away. There wasn't a soul for miles. No birds, no trees, just two climbers and a mountain of rock and ice.

The mountain is nameless. Climbers simply refer to it by its altitude: 11,300. It probably would have remained completely unknown to the rest of the world if it weren't for Steve House, one of America's premier mountaineers, who identified 11,300 as his favorite climb on the continent. That doubled the traffic on the mountain to about six climbers a year.

The only sensible way to climb a mountain like 11,300 is to move fast and light to beat the ever-approaching blizzards that are notorious in this part of Alaska. To stay light, we ditched all spares. No extra food. No extra clothes. One rope.

We started the climb by ascending a gully, a steep scar in the rock filled with waist-deep snow. We topped out of the gully and climbed along a ridge to ten thousand feet where we reached a notch. The only way across the notch was to rappel down seventy feet to a snowbank and then climb up the other side.

So here we are on the snowbank with the rope threaded through a metal ring above us. To continue up the mountain, we'll need the rope. If we pull the rope down, then there's no going back. The sheer seventy-foot wall we just rappelled down is unclimbable. The only way off the mountain will be to go up to the summit and then down the back side of the mountain.

The three most challenging sections of the mountain still lie above us: the narrow rock chimney nicknamed Thin Man's Squeeze, a razor-sharp ridgeline with a two-thousand-foot drop, and a final fifty-foot wall of ice to the summit.

It's 9:00 P.M. Snow is starting to fall. Decision time.

Most decisions made on any one day are utterly inconsequential. Paper or plastic? Grande or Venti? Red or white?

On those rare occasions when the decisions rise above the ordinary, they are typically hedged, safely reversible, buffered by a money-back guarantee or cushioned by a prenuptial agreement. And in Washington, D.C., where votes are regarded as the ultimate decision points, even those moments are lubricated by talking points that were tested by focus groups in Peoria.

That's why this moment, in a snowbank on a desolate Alaska

mountain, is so pure. And that's why I am drawn to this sport: it presents irreversible decisions. Either we pull the rope and continue up, with no chance for backtracking, or we haul ourselves back up the rope and go home. We have just a few moments to consider the situation, each of us silently evaluating the risks, balancing those against the opportunity to face the challenges.

I look up at the icy slope rising sharply above us, and pull the rope. I just committed us to going up into the night. Now this moment matters.

That is why I climb.

Unlike that moment in Alaska, this situation—standing in the glow of the jeep's headlights, surrounded by soldiers with guns at the ready—was totally outside my control. There was no rope that I could decide to pull or not pull. Instead, there were only triggers, and it was up to the soldiers, not me, to decide whether to pull them or not. This wasn't the kind of dramatic moment that I seek; this was utter helplessness.

Still, we didn't break down; we didn't plead. We just stared back into the eyes of the soldiers.

This isn't to say that we have ice in our veins. In fact, our steadiness at that moment shouldn't impress anyone. I think the reason we acted calmly was because we never really believed that violence would erupt. It hadn't the last time I stared down the barrel of a gun.

Years earlier I had visited the Dominican Republic with a friend who was on a work trip. While he was attending a business meeting, I explored Santo Domingo, wandering through the town and eventually into what appeared to be a mausoleum. A wall of etched plaques, each covering a space that could accommodate a casket, stood in front of me. A flame flickered nearby.

I heard someone call out and I turned. I remember focusing on his face before noticing that he had a rifle pointed at my head. Then he started yelling.

I'm half Ecuadorian, but that doesn't do any good since I can only speak English now. My mother spoke Spanish in the house; relatives who passed through our home spoke it on a regular basis. But I hadn't been immersed in Spanish in the decades since she had died.

I stared back at the guard, not comprehending.

He gave up on sentences and simplified his communication to what was the one essential word.

"Pantalones!" Still yelling, he lowered his rifle, pointing it at my knee.

There was no way he would blow my leg off. This had to be a simple misunderstanding; I was certain we would figure this out. The weapon was incidental, not really threatening, merely a means of getting my attention.

He began slamming the barrel of the rifle against my leg, just below the bottom of my shorts. I stared down at the rifle, confused. When I looked back up I noticed the crowd.

I wasn't alone in the building, but I was different from every other person there. I was wearing shorts, while everyone else had their legs covered in long pants or a skirt.

Okay, I got it: pants only, no shorts. I nodded at the guard and walked out, as calmly as I had walked in.

An incident like that informs future behavior, I suppose. And so, despite our trespassing in a gold mine at 2 A.M. and being surrounded by armed soldiers, I was reasonably calm because I had been through circumstances that led me to believe that situations like this do not erupt in violence. That would be crazy. The soldiers would use their guns to make their point, but the triggers would not be pulled. Nevertheless, something still had to be done. They were after something.

Perhaps the bribes we had provided earlier had not greased enough hands? Others who had heard about the bribes might now be angling to get a cut. Certainly, it was no secret that we were passing through the mine. We had spent an entire day hiding in the barracks on our way up and word of our presence surely got around the camp.

Expecting that the bribes were the core issue here, we offered the soldiers money. I don't recall having very much but we gave them what we had.

The yelling ceased; the soldiers parted. We got back in the jeep and drove on.

I remember shrugging off the incident at the time. It seemed like a dramatic way to squeeze us for whatever money we had left, but it appeared to be nothing more than that—just an ordinary shakedown.

A few days later we realized that far more had been at stake.

You can stand on the highest point on every continent but you can't surf every coastline. In fact, of the hundreds of thousands of miles of coast on the planet, only a small fraction is surfable. In most places, nature conspires against you.

The first requirement for surfing, of course, is that you need a wave, and you can't will a wave to roll in. Believe me, I've tried. I've been sitting on a surfboard, staring out at the ocean, floating on water as still and flat as a pane of glass, pleading for a wave to roll in. Nothing happens.

The waves that do roll in have a few possible sources. When wind blows over the ocean it creates waves. But wind waves are choppy, staggered, with no rhythmic pattern as they hit the shore. If waves were like music, then these would be the handiwork of a six-month-old with a tambourine: clatter and hash, nothing but noise. The best thing to do is let the child get it out of his system and wait for another day.

The ideal waves are created far out at sea, born of cyclones and hurricanes. Distant, intense, with powerful winds, these storms churn up the water, whipping up deep troughs in the ocean. As those troughs move out across the ocean on a journey taking them hundreds of miles toward land, they smooth out and get more rhythmic, transforming gradually into strong, steep, evenly spaced swells.

As the swells approach the shore, the ocean floor begins to shape the wave.

It is natural to think that only solids can be shaped and sculpted. Marble can be chiseled into a statue of David. Auguste Rodin extracted splendor out of bronze. Steel can be transformed into a Chrysler Building.

But who can sculpt a liquid? Humans can't. Nature can.

The ocean floor that rises up under the incoming swell acts as an artist's blade, carving and shaping the incoming water. The shore that the wave pours into confines it, limits it, like hands on the lump of clay spinning on a potter's wheel.

What finally arrives at the beach is not just water, it is contoured and rhythmic liquid. Born of violence, propelled a thousand miles by the fury of a storm, the wave is finally shaped in its final few hundred feet of travel, only to vanish and retreat in backwash.

The primary limiting factor to what coastline is surfable on this planet is the shore topography, the steepness of the ocean floor underneath the wave that does the sculpting in the final feet of its journey.

The reason a wave breaks is that the wall of water heading toward the beach starts to hit the slope of the shore. As the water swell hits that slope, it slows down. The water behind the swell is now moving slightly faster and it starts to pile up on top of the slower-moving water. The swell starts to curl. Eventually, as too much water starts to build up, the base can no longer sustain it and the wave breaks. The water at the top spills out over the front of the wave.

If a coastline is too steep, the waves break too close to the shore to accommodate any surfing. If the coastline is too shallow, the waves are nothing but gentle ripples, reaching the shore with only a quiet brushing of the sand. The gentle surf delights people with snorkels and tanning lotion, but it offers no pleasure to the surfer. The surfer has to search elsewhere for a wave.

In the best of all worlds, the incoming swell has a base-to-height ratio of two to one, creating a solid foundation to sustain the weight of the crest. The ideal coast will break the wave at a distance that allows a sustained ride to shore.

Those two restrictions massively reduce the amount of coastline available to surf. And once you've identified those locations on the planet with the perfect ocean topography, there remain still more complicating factors.

Waves that break over a reef would dice up the surfer, like being tossed onto a batch of kitchen knives. A rocky coastline isn't much better, though there are plenty of surfers willing to take the risk of getting tumbled around on coral and stones.

The wind can wreak havoc on the quality of the wave. Too much wind behind the wave, blowing toward shore, and the wave can get choppy or break too soon. Too much wind into the wave is no better. The ideal is just the right amount of wind blowing toward the shore, coupled with the right slope under the wave to create that perfect curl.

Even when you've identified the perfect topography, and you have a day with the ideal wind blowing at just the right speed and direction, you are still at the mercy of the weather. Nature has to do you the favor of serving up a storm out at sea.

Taking all those factors into account, the odds of randomly selecting a surfable beach is vanishingly small. It is more likely that you could win at Powerball than you could just put your thumb down on the coastline of a world map and ride a wave there on any given day.

Fortunately, surfers have combed the world for the right locations. One of the well-known spots is Bali, Indonesia, just a short hop from Papua, where we had been climbing.

There are dozens of surfing beaches to pick from on the island of Bali. Depending upon the time of year, surfers can find swells that are anywhere from two to twenty feet. With steady waves and reliable weather, the island hosts the occasional surfing competition. A competition means, of course, that there are gradations of skill levels among surfers that can be distinguished one from another.

Surfing breaks down into two generic types of maneuvers: functional and expressive. Functional moves are basic rotations and pivots that keep you riding the wave. Expressive moves, such as aerials that require the rider to rotate the board up over the wave and catch air, are like a gymnast's vault.

I'll confess, I'm no surfing star and I don't compete. Just as with my rock climbing and my mountaineering, I've learned to live with the fact that there is always someone else who is far better than me. They're faster, more nimble, more acrobatic, younger.

In my case, I'm satisfied with the steady, smooth ride of a long board. No aerials. I am compelled by the simplicity and purity of the sport. You don't have to pace out a field or raise a net. It doesn't require a club or bat, pads or spikes. No holes are dug, no contour smoothed, no rings hung. All you need is a board and a swimsuit, nothing more. It's as raw as that.

Better still, no one ever asks the question: why do you surf? That may be because the answer is so obvious; everyone understands, intuitively, without any need for explanation, why the sport is so appealing.

Surfing is so extraordinary, in fact, that it probably never occurred to the first people who saw a wave that they could actually ride it.

There are no cave drawings of surfers. And while the Mayans

had athletic fields and ancient Greece held Olympic games, the first documentation of a surfer came a millennium later in the pages of the journal of Lieutenant James King, who accompanied Captain Cook on his expedition sailing the Pacific Ocean. King, staring out at the locals on Kealakekua Bay, made this entry in the year 1779:

> *The Men lay themselves flat upon an oval piece of plank about their Size and breadth, they keep their legs close on top of it, and their Arms are us'd to guide the plank, they wait the time of the greatest Swell that sets on the Shore, and altogether push forward with their Arms to keep on its top, it sends them in with the most astonishing velocity, and the great art is to guide the plank so as always to keep it in proper direction on the top of the swell, and as it alters its direction.*
>
> *These men may be said to be almost amphibious.*

If walking on water was a miracle, then certainly taking a board and riding it on water must be something that all of us can, at the very least, appreciate as extraordinary.

That is why I surf.

And so, aspiring to be amphibious, a few days after driving out of the Freeport-McMoRan mine, with Puncak Jaya far behind us, I dropped a board into the surf of Kuta Beach, Bali. I had surfed before, but never was the moment as memorable as this time, when I stepped out of the water and my world was reshaped.

Most times when I'm on a climbing expedition or on a surfing trip I take a break from world news. This time, for no reason I can remember, while taking a breather from surfing, I picked up an international English-language newspaper and started flipping through it. In scanning the pages I saw a brief item about a group of American schoolteachers who were attacked in a bloody ambush. The details were still sketchy, the news still in flux, but it seemed that three people were killed and at least a few others wounded.

I suppose I might have turned the page with little notice, a tragedy certainly, but one with no particular connection to my life. But before I turned the page, I noticed where the massacre took place.

The Americans were murdered at the Freeport-McMoRan mine.

They had been traveling along the same road we had been on, just five hundred yards from the military base where we had been stopped. Their situation began, as it had for us, with gunmen confronting the vehicle.

The Freeport-McMoRan mine is a vast local enterprise employing nearly ten thousand people. A portion of those employees are foreign nationals, some of whom have school-age children. To accommodate their educational needs, the mine had established a school, bringing in highly qualified teachers.

A top-notch elementary school teacher can find a job in the United States without too much strain, even in the most difficult of economic times. Only a certain type of teacher would forgo those opportunities to take a job in Papua, Indonesia. They would need to be enticed by the distance from the industrialized world, curious about the culture, delight in travel, or perhaps be attracted to the lush biodiversity of the jungle.

Those interests were all shared by the teachers who filled the seats of the Land Cruisers that traveled north, along the mine road, on the morning of August 31, 2002. They had checked out of the military base, alerting the local authorities to their trip, and had been enjoying a day off from teaching by taking a day hike to explore the local ecology.

New Guinea has one of the most abundant ecosystems on the

planet. Nearly 10 percent of all known species live on the island, with many of them living nowhere else in the world. The numbers are truly astounding for an island: more than 200,000 species of insects and 20,000 species of plants. In any casual stroll through the jungles or valleys, a hiker would be guaranteed to see something unique in the world. That morning, the teachers had gone to see the tree frogs and orchids.

By late morning a light rain began falling and they went back to their Land Cruisers for the trip back up the mine road. With fog building up on the windows, in order to see out the side and back of the vehicles they had to wipe away the moisture with their palms, hands arcing across the glass, sweeping the jungle into view.

Rick Spier was driving the lead Land Cruiser, four fellow American teachers in the seats surrounding him. Ken Balk was following behind in a second Land Cruiser that carried his wife and daughter, two other American teachers, and the school's local Bahasa Indonesian teacher. Behind the two vehicles was a fuel tanker, making its way slowly up the mountain.

At 12:40 P.M., near milepost #62, a point just five hundred yards south of the military base, a group of gunmen confronted Spier's vehicle.

In our case, at or near that very same spot in the road, we came to a stop and our driver began shouting. In Spier's case, no words were passed. Bullets, dozens of them, started punching into Spier's vehicle.

When something is coming toward your face, the immediate reaction is to duck down and cover, shut your eyes and seek protection. Rick Spier didn't have that chance. The bullets came too fast; the attack was too sudden. He had no opportunity to shield himself. Rick Spier died instantly.

Sitting beside Spier was Ted Burgon, who was recently hired by the mine to be principal of the school. With the bullets coming in a spray across the front of the vehicle, there was no hope that anyone in the front seats could survive.

Ted Burgon was fatally shot.

With the driver lifeless, the Land Cruiser now veered to the left and crashed into an embankment. Three passengers were still alive, but there was now no hope of driving away from the scene. The metal doors offered no protection against the hail of bullets, the windshields were shattered; the passengers were encased in useless armor. If they stayed in place, they would certainly die.

Four minutes had passed since the massacre began. Ken Balk, driving the second Land Cruiser, had no idea what was going on up ahead, around the corner and out of view. He was about to steer his vehicle directly into the ambush.

As Balk turned the corner he saw the stalled vehicle in front of him. He hit the brakes on the Land Cruiser and came to a stop as the gunmen emerged from around Spier's vehicle. Balk's Cruiser came under immediate attack.

Bullets smacked into the sides of Balk's vehicle, slicing through the metal doors as if they were made of paper.

By this time, there had already been a staggering amount of shooting; nearly a hundred rounds of ammunition had already been fired against a group of people who were utterly defenseless. But the ambush wasn't even half over.

As the second Land Cruiser came to a stop, Patsy Spier, sitting in the backseat, caught a glimpse of the vehicle ahead of her. She couldn't see the driver, her husband.

Looking out the side window she noticed puffs of dirt lifting up off the ground, one after another, approaching the vehicle.

Patsy, not wearing her seat belt, pivoted to her side to get a clearer view and suddenly understood what was happening.

Bullets now shattered the front windshield and one pierced the left side of her back. The hollow point bullet exploded her eleventh rib, then splintered into pieces that stabbed into her kidney and surrounding organs. She threw herself down to the floor of the jeep.

Beside her sat Bambang Riwanto. His fingers were working the seat belt, but not quickly enough. By the time Riwanto unclipped, he was perforated with bullets. His dead body fell on top of Patsy, shielding her from the bullets that continued to stream into the vehicle.

For the passengers who survived the initial strafing, time now stretched out.

In the first Land Cruiser, the rear left passenger, Steve Emma, had taken bullets in his right shoulder, left leg, and hip. His body, he would describe later, felt like it was in flames from the searing shrapnel that tore through it.

With energy draining out of him, Emma kicked at the rear door of the Land Cruiser, bursting it outward. He now had a clear view of what was unfolding behind him.

All the passengers were realizing that the vehicles were death traps, offering no protection, keeping them pinned in place, fixed targets for the now roaming gunmen. Emma saw that three of the passengers from the rear Land Cruiser—Ken Balk, his wife, and their six-year-old daughter—had left the vehicle and were huddled behind the limited shielding of the rear tire. All three were bleeding. Balk was gushing blood from bullet wounds to his lumbar artery.

Patsy remained in the vehicle, nearly paralyzed by the shrapnel in her back and pinned down by the weight of Riwanto.

The surviving passengers tried communicating, shouting out to be heard over the sound of the gunfire.

"Gurus! Eskola Amerika! Bebe!" yelled one of the passengers. "Teachers! American school! Child!"

The appeal had no effect; the guns continued to pop, hammering into the bodies of one passenger after another.

Balk's daughter, now covered in her father's blood and bits of his tissue, asked why it wouldn't stop. There was nothing her parents could say or do to stop the bloodshed. It seemed the gunmen would walk up to each vehicle and pursue every passenger until they were all dead.

Patsy Spier accepted her fate. "I'm ready. It's okay, they can come and get me."

Bullets started punching through the back of the Land Cruiser and she felt one as it found its target, piercing her foot. In a few moments, only as long as it would take the shooters to sweep their rifles along the rear door, she knew she would be dead.

Patsy knew her husband was dead. She had heard shouting from the other vehicle, but did not hear his voice. If he were alive, he would have called out to her.

"Rick is gone. Just do it," she said, thinking that a shooter might come up to the window.

And then, there was a pause.

The fuel tanker now drove up into the chaos.

Rifles swung toward the tanker, bullets hammering across the cylinder of fuel and punching through the door of the cab. The cab sat higher off the ground than the Land Cruisers. The gunmen were shooting slightly up; they didn't have the clear sightline they had with Spier and Burgon.

The tanker turned across the length of the road, the cab coming to a stop near the front of Spier's Land Cruiser, the tank of fuel blocking passage. Fuel started to drip from the tank onto the dirt below.

Two dump trucks, traveling north along the road, rounded the corner and the shooters pivoted their rifles to the new targets.

The dump trucks now took the full fire of the gunmen. The ambush was now in its twentieth minute and rather than diminishing in intensity, more targets were being drawn in. So long as the shooters could keep every new arrival on the scene in their sights, the ambush would continue.

This was not a limited operation, tightly constrained in time or munitions. The gunmen walked calmly, deliberately, the plan open-ended, absorbing as many victims as the circumstances presented. They were indiscriminate in their bloodshed, unconcerned about the nature of the targets. Their rifles arced across mine vehicles and cars, their bullets aimed at men, women, and a child. Both Indonesians and Americans were targets.

With so many targets being drawn into the massacre, one would eventually get away.

Another car emerged, this one at the north end of the ambush, driven by a mine manager, Andrew Neale. The gunmen had been walking south, down the road, and were unable to spin around and get a clear shot at Neale's car a hundred feet behind them. Neale could see the carnage. He spun the wheel and U-turned back up the road, speeding toward the barracks to alert the soldiers.

The gunmen must have now realized the inevitable. Within minutes the Indonesian military would arrive in force and the shooters would confront the possibility of return fire. They dispersed.

A few minutes later, at approximately 1:10 P.M., the Indonesian military arrived.

The ambush had lasted nearly thirty minutes. In total, 234 bullet casings would be found on the scene amid the blood, bone, and tissue fragments. Two Land Cruisers and two dump trucks were punched full of bullets. A tanker trunk, the skin peeled back by bullets, dripped fuel oil.

By the time the military appeared, there was no one left for them to attack or arrest; the gunmen had apparently fled. The soldiers began to search for survivors.

As a soldier approached Patsy's vehicle, she remembered looking up at the gun slung over the shoulder, wanting to reach out to touch it. If it was warm, she thought, she would know that he was one of the shooters, a bad guy now posing as one of the good guys. Touching the barrel would have resolved so much of the confusion and accusations that were to follow, but she never got the chance.

Four soldiers stepped up, pulled back the perforated rear door, and lifted out Patsy's nearly lifeless body. She called out weakly, barely audible, for her husband. There was no answer. She knew there would never be a reply from him again.

It was too rainy and foggy to land a helicopter on the narrow road, so the survivors were driven to the mining camp hospital for triage until they could be evacuated to a fully equiped medical facility for emergency surgery. As the jeep bounced along, Patsy asked, "What's the date today?"

The doctor was surprised. "Why, is it someone's birthday?"

She replied, one of the last things she remembered before drifting into a morphine haze:

"It's the day my husband died."

Three people were killed in the ambush, eleven wounded. Several of them were wounded so severely that their survival was in question. Patsy Spier, near death, was flown to a specialty clinic in Australia. An incision was made in her abdomen and all the internal organs were extracted from her body and tweezed on an operating table in an attempt to remove the shards of splintered bullets. Seventy pieces of shrapnel would remain in her left side and kidney; removing them proved to be too dangerous.

Within hours of the shootings, the army declared that the crime was the work of an armed separatist group, the Organisasi Papua Merdeka (OPM), or Free Papua Movement, which aspired to create an independent state in West Papua. The OPM had been active in the mine, the military asserted, and there was clear evidence that they were looking for a high-profile target.

Over the next three months, the case became murkier. An alternative explanation began to emerge. A careful examination of the scene suggested that the Indonesian military itself may have been involved in the massacre. The *Washington Post* ran the story in early November:

Indonesia Military Allegedly Talked of Targeting Mine

Sunday, November 3, 2002

By Ellen Nakashima and Alan Sipress

Washington Post Foreign Service

JAKARTA, Indonesia, Nov. 2—Senior Indonesian military officials discussed an operation against Freeport-McMoRan Copper & Gold Inc. before an ambush near its mine in Papua province that killed two Americans and one Indonesian on Aug. 31, according to intelligence obtained by the United States, a U.S. government official and other sources said.

The discussions involved the top ranks of Indonesia's military . . . and were aimed at discrediting a Papuan separatist group, the Free Papua Movement, said the U.S. government official and another American source.

The attack took place near a mine operated by New Orleans–based Freeport; the three victims were contract employees. The intelligence was based on information supplied after the ambush by a person who claimed to be knowledgeable about the high-level military conversations. The source was described in the report as "highly reliable." This information was supported by an intercept of a conversation including that individual, said the U.S. government official and the American source. The intercept was shared with the United States by another country, identified by a Western source as Australia.

The Ambush

Subordinates could have understood the discussions as a direction "to take some kind of violent action against Freeport," the government official said.

The two radically different explanations of the ambush did have one thing in common. An armed group, whether guerrilla or Indonesian military, had been planning to attack someone passing along the mine road in August of 2002. They were looking for victims. Given the nature of the massacre, anyone would have served their purpose.

Gunmen had stepped out in front of my vehicle, they had stepped out in front of Spier's vehicle. For whatever reason, they did not pull their triggers in my case. So, despite the claims and counterclaims of who initiated the attack, there was one thing that I knew for sure: I dodged the attack that Patsy Spier later took.

I remember that moment sitting on the beach in Bali, staring at the paper in disbelief. It was still months before I would learn the details of the attack, see the police reports, and feel compelled to act. For now, I was just processing the shock.

"What's up?" Mike asked.

"You're not going to believe this," I said, and explained what I had just read in the newspaper.

Later that day I would explain it all again, to Gina, who had planned to meet me, post-climb, on the sands of Kuta Beach. As we talked about the ambush, a string of unanswerable questions came to mind.

"What if we hadn't offered more money on our way back down the mine road?"

Before Gina could respond, I fired off another question: "What if we had waited a couple more days to do the climb?"

"Then it could have been you instead of them," Gina said. "So, are you wondering why it wasn't you?" she asked.

I knew what was coming.

"Sometimes," she observed, "things just turn out this way."

"Oh c'mon, Gina. Don't tell me this happened for a reason. You know I don't buy that."

In response, she added a question of her own: "Okay, so what are the chances of it happening? Remember how unlikely it was that we met. You figured out the odds."

The likelihood that I would be at that particular milepost that very week was small; Gina was right about that.

"I don't believe in fate, Gina." I don't accept that an event can somehow be hardwired into life, so that no one has control over it. She knew my perspective—a perspective she didn't share.

"There must be something that you think of that can happen for a reason." She wasn't insistent, just curious. It seemed obvious to her that this event should be challenging my worldview.

"When there's a reason, science can explain it," I responded. "Anything else is just coincidence."

She stopped short of suggesting that destiny played a role in the events that unfolded at the Freeport-McMoRan mine. Instead, she closed with a question. "So what's your explanation this time? I guess you think you just got lucky."

I look back now and still more questions come to mind.

What if I hadn't picked up the paper that morning? I might never have noticed the story and the next few years of my life would have taken a completely different direction.

What if we had climbed that mound, Mount Kosciuszko in Australia, instead of the peak in Oceania?

What if . . . What if . . . What if . . .

Events were put in motion that day. My simple surfing and climbing plan was about to get extraordinarily complicated. I was about to get entangled in the life of one of the survivors of the ambush. And, as utterly improbable as it sounds, she would eventually be working a job in an office just a few hundred yards from me in Washington, D.C.

"You sound like a horse when you eat like that," Gina says with a laugh from across the table as I'm crunching down a bowl of cereal. We only have about four hours until we need to be at the airport and we're downing a quick breakfast. At the moment, we don't have any plans for how we're going to spend the time.

"What are you going to do?" Gina asks.

We were heading back to the U.S. from Indonesia and had laid over in Vietnam on the way. We had this last morning in Hanoi.

"I'm going to the Ho Chi Minh Mausoleum. Want to come?"

Gina looked back at me with complete disinterest. I could tell from her expression that she couldn't imagine anything more boring.

"You're going to see a dead guy?"

I gave the mausoleum the best defense I could think of. "They keep him in a glass case. He's been there for decades and I'm wondering what he looks like."

"He'll look dead, Slake. It's not like you can talk to him or kick him in the ass. For all you know it's just a wax figure. Who cares?"

There's a science to the preservation of a body. Egyptians developed a method to preserve bodies, mummies, intact for millennia without any need for attention. Ho Chi Minh's body, on the other hand, was under careful daily surveillance for any signs of decay. I was curious how the two techniques compared. But I could see that none of that was going to persuade Gina. "So what are you going to do?"

"I don't know yet. I'll fill you in when I meet you at the airport. We'll see who has the better time."

I arrived at the mausoleum a half hour later and with assembly line efficiency I was directed into an enormous stream of Vietnamese, all of us now moving toward a five-story-tall tiered structure of gray granite blocks. The thick crowd was narrowed to a precise single file as we entered the building and began a slow hour-long march toward a guarded room ahead of us.

As I entered the room, I felt cool air blow across my back. Something in here was definitely being kept on ice, preserved and chilled. But this didn't have the frigid feel of a Himalayan peak; that would have been familiar, comfortable. No, this was different, a chill that someone, something, could never thaw from.

At the room's center was an elevated glass casket. Long thin velvet tubes connected a series of pedestals that established our path toward and around the casket.

A guard was calling out a few words over and over and over again in a steady rhythmic tone, like a drumbeat. As I approached the glass, he looked at me and converted the Vietnamese chant into English. "Keep moving. Keep moving. Keep moving."

And then the embalmed body came into view.

Flat on his back, clothed with only his head and hands visible, lay the former leader of Vietnam. The soft dim light on his face illuminated the skin; his cheeks looked a bit flush. He seemed serene, but not asleep. It appeared like he'd just gotten back from a brisk walk and was now lying down peacefully to catch his breath.

As I exited the room, with the guard's steady rhythmic demand now fading behind me, only one thought came to my mind: that was a waste of time. Gina was going to have a better story.

The airport was crowded, but Gina was easy to spot, the only Italian among the sea of Asians.

"So, how was it? Seeing the dead guy," she asked as I walked up.

"Not very interesting. What did you do?"

"I got a massage in the home of a blind masseuse. I found her place while I was wandering around downtown."

I stared back at Gina. "I can't beat that," I admitted. I had consorted with the dead; she was immersed in life.

That moment exposed the core of our relationship. Sure, we had a surprising amount in common: both of us raised through our teens by a single parent, both the youngest of three siblings, both of us moving across the country for high school, both losing a close family member to cancer. But those similarities weren't the glue in our relationship. Our relationship stuck because of our independence, our tolerance for each other to go along separate paths.

When we were at the same place at the same time and had a chance to choose our own course, we went in entirely different directions. Yet, hours later, we ended up at precisely the same spot, standing together, comfortably side by side, about to ride a plane home.

Gina had been through so much of what I had been through, but unlike me she never iced over. Looking back at me that afternoon in the airport, she knew that I thought her story was more appealing than mine. She also sensed that the events in Indonesia would change me. She didn't have to wait long.

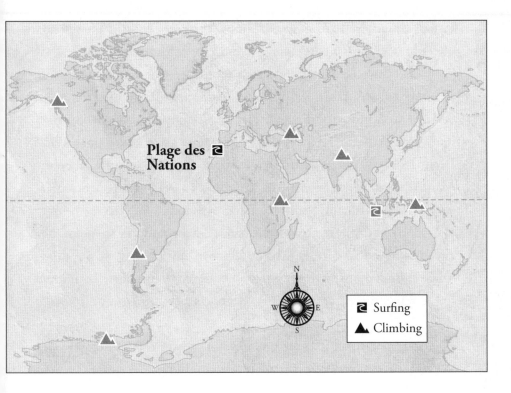

Plage des Nations

🏄 Surfing
⛰ Climbing

Chapter 7

SHARED PURPOSE

The hallway is an obstacle course, filing cabinets and boxes lining the walls, probably jammed with the results of previous congressional investigations. I am led through the maze to a conference room and stand waiting in front of it. Hundreds of people have walked down this corridor and pushed open this very door. Some entered hoping for justice, others, perhaps guilty or simply cautious, entered silently and offered no answers, taking refuge behind the Fifth Amendment.

I walk into the stark windowless room and take a seat on one side of a long wooden table. Sitting opposite me are staff on the Homeland Security Committee of the House of Representatives. They will pepper me with questions, I expect this, and I will answer every one as best I can. I will tell them what I know about the shooters, the Freeport-McMoRan mine, milepost #62. I have also read the police reports about the ambush and I will share my suspicions.

I don't have a lawyer with me, since I have nothing to hide. They already know that I trespassed and bribed my way across the mine. Those indiscretions have been public knowledge ever since I admitted to them in a piece I wrote for the *Washington Post* about my climb and the ambush.

I never expected that my pursuit of a surfing and climbing record would lead me to this room. At the beginning of my quest, I would never guess that I would care enough about a stranger's life or about international politics to get involved. Yet here I am, staring into the faces of the congressional staff, willing to answer questions and be part of a solution.

Gina is waiting for me at home, eager to hear the outcome. And the amulet, that preposterous amulet, is still stuffed into the back of my sock drawer. It wouldn't be there much longer.

By the time I returned to the United States from Bali, the ambush had made international headlines. The ramifications for U.S.-Indonesian relations were enormous.

It had been less than a year since the collapse of the Twin Towers and in the post-9/11 world, President George W. Bush was evaluating which countries could be relied on to join the battle against terrorists.

Indonesia was probably circled in red on the map in the Pentagon war room.

Indonesia is the largest Muslim country in the world and there were reports of terrorist groups training in the jungles of some of the remote islands. But with accounts of possible Indonesian soldiers' involvement in the ambush, a question was emerging. Could the Indonesian military be trusted to combat the terrorists? There was only one way to know for sure.

The White House dispatched a team of FBI investigators to Papua in late 2002 to investigate the ambush. By February of 2003, Congress received intelligence reports that said there was a "strong possibility" that Indonesian soldiers were the murderers. One theory was that the soldiers arranged the ambush to create chaos, then they planned to squeeze the mine for more money to combat the very chaos they had created.

That theory didn't sound far-fetched to me. After all, I knew that some of the soldiers were corrupt. I was counting on it when we bribed them. Also, having interacted with those soldiers, I had no trouble believing they could have gunned people down without blinking.

The FBI investigation was incomplete; there was nothing conclusive, no hard evidence to indicate that the Indonesian military was involved in the ambush. At the same time, the need to confront potential terrorist training grounds in Indonesia was perceived to be necessary and immediate. That presented a challenging decision.

The Bush administration made the tough call: fund the Indonesian military.

I recognize that was a difficult decision, still, I disagreed with it. Perhaps I could overlook the ambush—if the military was in fact involved—for the sake of the battle against terrorists if it were an isolated incident, one act by a rogue element. But the Indonesian military's human rights abuses stretch back decades. In fact, that very month, eighteen defendants, mostly Indonesian soldiers, were on trial for participating in a wave of killings, lootings, and rapes in the province of East Timor.

It may seem hypocritical that I would disagree with the administration's decision to fund the Indonesian military, given that I had funded members of the Indonesian military myself. To pass through the mine, I placed stacks of bills into the open palms of soldiers. I admit that my payout was intended simply to achieve my own personal ambition, nothing so righteous as paying to combat terrorists and protect U.S. citizens. I accept that criticism. But it didn't change my conclusion.

I believed that the ambush had to be fully investigated; the survivors deserved at least that much. And there was another reason to investigate it more thoroughly: if the Indonesian military was involved in the ambush, then they couldn't be trusted to be allies in combating terrorists. In fact, if they pulled triggers on Americans, they were terrorists themselves.

As I saw it, U.S. funding for training the Indonesian military was the only leverage the United States had. I concluded that the U.S. should suspend those funds until the ambush investigation was complete.

What I did next still surprises me to this day. I dropped that vow I made not to write about my travels; I sent an article to the *Washington Post,* spilling my entire Freeport story.

I had helped people before, of course, in small ways, doing things that would not particularly inconvenience me. The opinion piece for the *Post* was different.

I didn't know the survivors of the ambush; I owed them nothing. Confessing to my bribes and trespassing could open me up to criminal charges, I supposed. Challenging the U.S. government decision to support the Indonesian military would probably bring me nothing but hate mail. I had plenty of reasons not to write that piece.

I can only explain why I did it this way: my journey had now changed. This was no longer a self-absorbed quest. The climbing and surfing record had taken me in an unexpected direction. The sensory deprivation tank of Antarctica had put an end to my detachment from the world. The ambush in Indonesia would push me further into it.

I no longer have that first e-mail message from her, but I remember when I received it. A few days after my article was published in the *Post,* I sat, frozen in my chair, staring at an unopened message in my computer's inbox. It was an e-mail from Patsy Spier, one of the survivors of the ambush.

From the moment the article appeared, I was blasted with criticism from people who thought that I was jeopardizing the ability of the U.S. to effectively combat terrorism. The only interesting thing that had come out of all this was that I had been sent, confidentially, a copy of the classied police report on the ambush investigation. The report was clear—there was good reason to be wary of the Indonesian military—but it was no help in my responding to people whose minds were made up.

Amid these fuming e-mails, Spier's message arrived.

I didn't open it right away. I sat back in my chair, questions coming to mind. Was she offended by my article? Would she be angry that I had brought the ambush back into the media? Maybe she preferred that the public attention would go away so she could move past it and get on with her life. Perhaps she would regard my behavior at the mine as reckless, that I was an enabler, encouraging the bad behavior of the military? Now I saw only downsides to the opinion piece, none of which had occurred to me until that very moment.

I leaned forward in my chair and clicked open Spier's message.

———

There are people in this world who, against all odds, press on. They are vigorous, despite having seventy shards of metal perforating their internal organs. They are calm, even when they have a rifle barrel pointed at them, a whisker away from death. They are engaging and warm and determined, despite having every reason in the world to be consumed by hatred. Such is Patsy Spier.

I blow into my coffee, cooling it off for a sip. Across from me, green eyes blazing, sits Patsy Spier. She sits upright, not stiff or tense, simply poised, confident, with a presence that comes from spending an afternoon in the company of death. She is waiting for me to put the cup down before she speaks; she wants my full attention.

Her e-mail had simply asked to meet with me, since she would be in Washington the following week. I accepted the offer and here we are meeting for the first time. In the next few seconds I would find out what she thinks of me.

"Thank you," she says.

To this day, I don't think that opinion piece I wrote deserved a thank-you. Yet she said it nevertheless. She went on to explain why she was in town: she was trying to get members of Congress to suspend funding to the Indonesian military until the investigation was complete.

I agreed with her, of course. But I thought to myself: what more can I do about it? The odds of halting the federal funding to Indonesia seemed insurmountable. I had written the article, I had delivered my opinion, and I was done. This wasn't my fight.

Then she said a few more words, penetrating words, and everything changed.

"I want to see the shooters hunted down. But I'm not doing this for me." She looked at me, unblinking, eyes fixed. With absolute conviction, she explained to me her reason, her deeper motivation.

"I'll do whatever I can to keep someone else from suffering the way we did."

Those words froze me. This was not about vengeance, although she had every right for it to be. She wasn't seeking payback or retribution. She wanted the killers found and removed, certainly, but not for her own sake. She was fighting for others: she had humanity.

And then I thought about myself.

What was the point of my post-Antarctica desire to connect with the world if it was only for my own sake, if I was still so self-absorbed?

Evolution is usually gradual. It took 600 million years for creatures to grow, develop, deepen their capabilities, and then claw their way out of the depths, struggle into the sun, and take their first full breath of air. That very evolution occurred in me over my decadelong journey, but much of it would happen now, at this very moment, as Patsy Spier's words sank in.

My surfing and climbing record served no purpose beyond my own self-satisfaction. Now I had the opportunity to engage in something far larger than myself and I was invigorated by it. I was compelled to participate more deeply. This was something beyond my own self-interest; Patsy and I had a shared purpose. I would warm to a more human temperature, a temperature at which the ground softens, and pillars start to teeter and fall.

There will be readers at this point who think I have lost my way.

What does the ambush have to do with surfing and climbing?

Nothing.

What does the ambush have to do with what my journey had become?

Everything.

Three years earlier I would have ignored these events, never turned on my computer to write that opinion piece for the *Post,* never have sat before congressional staff testifying to what I saw. Instead, I would have turned my head and continued down the list, planning the next ocean to surf.

Why the change?

As I listened to Patsy that day I realized what had been in the back of my mind since the afternoon on the beach in Bali when I opened that paper and saw the story of the ambush. I had dodged a bullet, and I was now looking at the person who took it, full in the back.

Yes, I had plenty of near misses before, but never one where someone else took the hit instead. It could have been Mike and me in that ambush; and becoming aware of that fact bent my life.

That conversation with Patsy Spier changed me. It had to.

Some people are born with a deep concern for the welfare of others; I was not. For them, taking action on someone else's behalf is a no-brainer. Of course, they would think, you do what you can for the survivor of the ambush and you say what you know to congressional investigators. But not me.

I had to experience the near miss and meet the person who suffered in my place before I developed the sensitivity to get involved and get outside myself.

Every culture and creed has its way of explaining a moment like that. For the religious, as the sixteenth-century preacher John Bradford said while watching a prisoner walk to his execution: "There but for the grace of God go I." There are plenty of other ways of conveying the same point.

In Farsi, the phrase is "*Ghesser dar raftan.*"

In Spanish: "*Se salvó por un pelo.*"

In Italian: "*Per il rotto della cuffia.*"

For me, it is simply this: I dodged a bullet.

"So who did it?" the staffer from the Homeland Security Committee asks from across the table.

I pause before responding, reminding myself of the way I had planned to address that very question. "How about I walk you through the evidence? I'll tell you what I know—the forensics, the bullets, the clues—and then I'll tell you what I think it all means."

The staff nod their approval. I start with the motives.

The OPM had been seeking independence from Indonesia since 1965. Claiming to have no cultural or geographic ties to Indonesia, they established their own flag and guerrilla army. They gained support among the indigenous population, due in large part to their opposition to the Freeport-McMoRan mine.

The guerrilla force is poorly equipped and vastly outnumbered by the Indonesian military. In order to get visibility for their cause and demonstrate that they are a force to be reckoned with they needed a strike against high-profile targets. At the time of the ambush, according to various sources, the OPM was looking for precisely that; it wanted to put a target in its crosshairs that would get it international attention.

All of the assembled congressional staff accept that motive. It's the story that we all want to be true. If the ambush was all the OPM's doing, it would simplify the decisions on who the U.S. should ally with in combating terrorists. Unfortunately, things weren't so straightforward.

Implicating the Indonesian military was touchy and I didn't want what I was about to say next to hang just on my word. So I had brought with me an investigative article from the *New York Times*.

U.S. Links Indonesian Troops to Deaths of 2 Americans

By Raymond Bonner

New York Times

JAKARTA, Indonesia, Jan. 29—Bush administration officials have determined that Indonesian soldiers carried out a deadly ambush that killed two American teachers returning from a picnic in a remote area of Indonesia last August, senior administration officials say.

The Indonesian military has denied any involvement in the ambush, which also killed an Indonesian teacher and wounded eight Americans. But a report by the country's police force last year suggested that the military was behind the killings.

The administration official and diplomats from other countries said there was still a mystery about who ordered the killings and why. They said the most likely explanation was that soldiers were trying to send a message to the teachers' employer, an American company that operates one of the world's largest copper and gold mines in the area. The company, Freeport-McMoRan Copper & Gold, had reduced payments and other benefits to soldiers, the officials said.

"Extortion, pure and simple," said a Western intelligence analyst, explaining what he believed was behind the attack.

Money from Freeport may have been the motivation. A soldier's pay is roughly $15 a month, the report says, adding that soldiers have "a high expectation" when they get assigned to the Freeport area. But they had been disappointed by what they received, and some "perks" had been reduced.

The Indonesian military receives less than one third of its budget from the government. To make up the difference, it relies on its own business activities as well as supplements from foreign businesses, especially natural-resource companies.

Freeport had begun to reduce these payments, on the advice of company lawyers who said they would have to be disclosed under new American corporate-responsibility laws, Western officials and people close to the company said. They also said the military wanted a portion of payments—1 percent of profits—that Freeport makes for community projects, part of its effort to improve local relations.

That pressure was apparently on the increase: investigators say they have been told that, in the weeks before the attack, Freeport had received threats of retaliation from the military if more money was not forthcoming.

So at the time of the ambush, the Freeport-McMoRan mine had begun cutting back on payments to the Indonesian military. The mine reduced perks, salaries, and the number of troops. An ambush at the mine against high-profile targets would demonstrate the need for a strong, sizable military presence and would likely restore those cuts. Clearly, the military had a plausible motive, just like the OPM.

I summarize it this way to the staff: "Both the OPM and the Indonesian military had reasons to carry out the attack."

With that established, I turn to the hard evidence and what I had intuited, starting with the guns and shells.

According to U.S. State Department documents, some of the weapons that were used during the ambush were Steyr AUG assault rifles. That rifle fires 5.56mm rounds and ninety-four of those very shell casings were found at the scene of the ambush. The Steyr rifle, as it turns out, is a weapon of the Indonesian military and not in the arsenal of the Free Papua Movement.

Ninety-four Steyr shells were found scattered on the ground, but more rounds were fired than that. Investigators walked through the entire scene, attempting to reconstruct the ambush bullet by bullet. The dozens of holes punched through the sides of the jeep and fuel truck were easy to add up, but there were countless additional rounds that had shattered glass, torn through tires and trees, laying waste to the surroundings but eluding the count. At minimum, the investigators determined, two hundred and thirty four rounds were fired.

"At least two hundred bullets," I repeat, pausing over the number. "That's a clue in itself."

The Free Papua Movement has few resources. All of their previous assaults were small-scale, using only a handful of bullets, conserving what limited supplies of ammunition they had. That, according to one of the investigators, suggested that it was highly unlikely that they would use hundreds of rounds in a single operation. "The group does not have the quantity of bullets," the investigator concluded.

And then there is the issue of time. Previous guerrilla attacks were quick, limited strikes, lasting only a few minutes. With the Freeport ambush taking place just five hundred yards from a military base, you might expect that the shooters would be quick, the operation brief to allow them to flee the scene before the army arrived. But that wasn't the case; the ambush lasted half an hour. And rather than a limited strike, the shooters expanded the attack, engaging more targets as they arrived on the scene.

And what about credit? Don't most terrorists boast about attacks so they can generate the attention and public fear that they're after?

In fact, the Free Papua Movement had a history of taking credit for their assaults. But in the case of the Freeport mine, with the bloody ambush receiving international attention that brought a high profile to whoever was responsible, the guerrillas denied any involvement. No one took credit for the attack.

"All of that evidence is compelling, but it's all circumstantial," I say to the congressional staff.

While together it suggests that the Indonesian military was involved, the clues could each be explained in other ways. The guerrillas could have acquired the Steyr rifles and ammunition in a raid of a military barracks. They could have determined that a high-profile target required the use of a larger portion of their ammunition. They could have changed their typical strategy, lengthening the time of attack for the Freeport assault.

At this point, it seemed the case could be argued either way; nothing tipped the scale. But I wasn't done.

"There's one more piece of evidence."

Everything I have said up to this point could be intuited from newspaper reports and TV coverage of the ambush. But I had something more, something that was not publicly available; I had a copy of the classified police report. It was delivered to me after my article appeared in the *Washington Post*. The report contained one additional, critical piece of evidence.

"Another body was found at the scene."

For nearly twenty-four hours after the ambush, no bullets had been fired at milepost #62, in the heart of the Freeport-McMoRan mine. Investigators had paced through the destruction, counting shells and attempting to reconstruct the massacre.

Now soldiers were patrolling the crime scene, safeguarding the evidence for the continued investigation.

At 11:40 A.M., the sound of three rifle shots broke the silence.

Within hours, the scene was again filled with investigators. The Papua police chief, Major General Pastika, arrived to find a dead body. Standing beside it was an army corporal, one of the soldiers patrolling the scene.

The soldier explained that he spotted an armed Free Papua Movement guerrilla walking along the cliffside above. Realizing that his life was in danger, he had lifted his rifle and shot, firing off three rounds. They were direct hits; the guerrilla fell from the cliff, his lifeless frame entangled in the vines of the jungle floor. With the help of fellow soldiers, he hauled the body out and onto the nearby road.

Pastika examined the body but found no identification. He called it "Mr. X."

Mr. X was clearly a native Papuan. Criminals return to the scene of the crime, the Indonesian military officers explained to Pastika, and that is precisely what Mr. X had done. This body, the officers insisted, is all the evidence that was needed. It proved that the guerrillas, the Free Papua Movement, had committed the ambush.

But Pastika continued to examine the body. He discovered that there was no blood flowing from the three bullet wounds. There were no broken bones, despite the fall from the cliff. The body was stiff, surprisingly so; he tried to reposition it but the hands couldn't be folded. The military's story was beginning to unravel.

Pastika transferred the body to the hospital and ordered an autopsy.

The forensic specialist, Dr. Agung, found small larvae in the body. Those larvae acted as a stopwatch, their growth an indication of the very moment of death. The evidence was now inescapable. Mr. X had been killed much earlier than 11:40 that morning, hours before the corporal claimed to have shot him.

Agung then discovered that Mr. X suffered from an acute and debilitating form of hydrocele. With that health condition, he concluded, Mr. X could never have walked up the hill to the cliffside.

On news of the autopsy results, Pastika returned to milepost #62. He walked to the very spot where the corporal claimed to have shot Mr. X. As he looked up from that spot, he was surprised by what he saw. The jungle was dense with foliage: the cliff wasn't visible. The soldier could never have had a clear shot from this position.

Pastika has a reputation of being deliberate and objective in his investigations, and he didn't rush to judgment in this case. Weeks went by as he assembled the facts and absorbed all the evidence available. He was fully aware of the risks of implicating the Indonesian military.

So much of the evidence could be argued either way. But one piece of evidence spoke to Pastika with clarity. As he finalized the classified police report, he identified the only conclusion one can reasonably draw from the appearance of the unexpected corpse:

EVALUATION ANALYSIS

It is the most possible scenario that has been proposed. Mr. X was shot to death before. Then Mr. X's dead body was brought and placed on the side of the road in order to "invite" the police investigator team to come and to investigate the location of the incident and at the same time to . . . witness that Mr. X was the attacker on August 31, 2002.

The story was phony. The military had tried to set Pastika up.

"You asked me who did it," I say to the congressional staff after describing Pastika's analysis and his final report entry.

"I don't know for sure who did it, I probably never will, but I do know this: there's enough evidence for the U.S. to suspend funding the Indonesian military until the investigation is complete."

The conference room is silent.

A congressional staffer, a close friend of mine, had led me into the room and sat beside me during the discussion. She was the first one to speak:

"I think that's all, right, Slake?"

It was. I had no idea how long I'd been talking, but I was drained, utterly depleted. I had nothing more to say. We got up and left the room. Later, reflecting back on that moment, that staffer, my close friend, told me what she thought. "That was your humanizing moment, Slake."

"What do you mean?" I had no idea what she was referring to.

"When you were in that room, going through all that evidence, it wasn't about you. It was about someone else. You cared. You cared about Patsy Spier; you cared about others."

I left that hearing room and it was then, and only then, that I went back to my surfing and climbing To Do List.

It was time to surf the Atlantic Ocean; after being consumed by the ambush for months I needed the break. I just needed to find a way to make it an interesting surf trip.

I had never surfed the east coast of the United States and doing it now seemed a bit unsatisfying. I had to get away. Gina had a suggestion. She had some friends who lived in the Dadès Gorge, an oasis in the Sahara desert. We could visit them and, along the way, I could surf the coast of Morocco.

"Great idea," I told her. "Just one question: does Morocco have waves?"

For centuries, the search for waves was a low-tech endeavor. If you were wondering whether there were waves to surf, you had to walk down to the beach, hold your hand over your eyes to block the glare of the sun, and check for yourself. The only innovation that intruded on that ritual was a pair of sunglasses.

Times have changed.

Surf forecasting has gone high-tech. Before you even pull on a swimsuit, you can log on the Web and get reliable wave predictions at nearly every surfable beach in the world.

The Web sites rely on information beamed from several sources.

Shared Purpose

Initially, there was NASA's QuikSCAT satellite. The core of the orbiting 450-pound beast was a rotating dish antenna that emitted two pulsed microwave beams, sweeping in circular patterns that cover a broad swath of the earth's surface. It beamed out a measurement of wind speed and wind direction roughly every 0.3 second. When a Titan II rocket blasted it into the sky in 1999, its purpose was to put the earth's climate under a microscope and provide a steady stream of data that could inform weather forecasting. When it was devised, no scientist thought that surfers would be one of its consumers. Now it's obvious that surfers were bound to benefit from satellites that provided detailed information on ocean behavior.

QuikSCAT was eventually replaced by five geosynchronous satellites that currently provide detailed pictures of weather patterns as they form and move across the globe. These workhorses sit in stationary positions relative to the earth nearly 24,000 miles over our heads, always staring down at the same vast patch of the globe, a constant eye on the activity of the Atlantic, Pacific, Indian, and Arctic Oceans. We've all seen these satellites at work, beaming back images of a froth of clouds whipping up into hurricanes, like Katrina, that hurtle toward the Southeast coast of the United States.

These instruments provide detailed imagery of swells as well as information on developing storms, their intensity, and their direction. All of that can then be fed into computer models to give surfers the information they really want: wave height and wave frequency. In other words: How big? How often?

The forecasts of height and frequency are outputs of the WaveWatch 3 computer model, managed by the U.S. government's National Oceanic and Atmospheric Administration—NOAA. While the surfer is still dozing, before the sun has even come up, the NWW3 software is grinding through millions of calculations per second to determine wave propagation across the earth's oceans.

The input to the NWW3 computer model comes not just from satellites, but also buoys, ships, weather stations, and airplanes sampling across the globe. The info determines wave height and frequency at the beach with high accuracy. It can even project out four to five days, although, just like any weather forecast, accuracy declines the further out in the future the projections are made.

Even with all this data and modeling, there are surfers who want to see the wave before making a decision. In that case, the surfer still doesn't have to leave home. Numerous beaches boast "surfcams," accessible over the Web, to save a surfer the trouble of having to walk down to the beach and get sand between the toes.

Despite all of this technology, despite the up-to-the-minute ocean conditions and coastal details that are available, it is still up to the surfer to catch the wave. For that to happen, in order to ride a wave, a surfer must, literally, become one with nature. That sounds so ridiculous it requires some explaining.

In order to ride liquid a surfer must get the speed of the board to match the speed of the incoming wave. If you paddle too fast, you outrun the wave. If you paddle too slowly, the wave moves out from under you and passes you by.

But when you paddle at just the right speed, when your board speed matches the speed of the wave, a remarkable thing happens: you are taken up by the wave. You can feel the very moment through the board when your speed and the wave's speed are in sync; then, you stop paddling, stand up, and ride the wave to shore. You are literally lifted and carried by the water, propelled by nature, part of it.

That experience, surfing's harmony with nature, is the antithesis of high altitude mountain climbing.

Climbing is a battle, every step a push against nature. Gravity tugs down on your boots, resisting their pull out of the snow. It drags at you, taunts you, whispers in your ear that you can't possibly get any higher, that you should turn around and go home. And in the meantime the storm blinds your vision and the wind whips at your skin. To survive in that environment, you need to be encased in gear, limiting all exposure to the elements, restricting nature's ability to freeze you on the spot.

Compare that experience to surfing.

With surfing, the storm is your companion and gravity is your ally. The storms churn up the perfect swells far out at sea that become smooth and periodic as they move toward the coast. Gravity collapses the incoming swell, creates the curl, and pulls you down and forward; you literally drop into the trough of the wave.

Yvon Chouinard, a king of El Cap rock climbing, is also a surfer. He once said he thought that surfing and climbing were a perfect pairing of sports because they are both equally useless. That's true. But there is also this: climbing and surfing are the yin and yang of athletic endeavors. One is in a battle with nature; the other is in harmony with it. One manages the mountains, the other the troughs.

At one time in my life I was yin-less. Only the battle, the isolated struggle and disconnection, appealed to me. But things changed. After experiencing the pure deprivation of Antarctica, after dodging a bullet in Indonesia, harmony now had appeal.

In Morocco, I found that harmony on a beach called Plage des Nations. The surfing there couldn't have been any more peaceful. Getting around the country, however, was a battle that almost cost Gina and me our lives.

The radio is at full volume as we round the turn, the driver talking at the top of his voice, yelling to us over the sounds of the blaring Arab music.

We found Hassan, the driver, in the coastal town of Essaouira and negotiated a bargain price for him to take us over the Atlas Mountains of Morocco to our friends who lived in the Dadès Gorge, at the western end of the Sahara.

A driver would be quicker and cheaper than taking a bus. The problem, we now realize, is that you get what you pay for. Our driver is evidently clinically insane.

"I'm four-star driver," he screams over his shoulder. "The best."

Hassan is a hulk. His body fills the front seat like it's an undersized suit, his left shoulder nearly touching the glass of the door window. He leans slightly forward making it look like the entire car is too small to contain him. The steering wheel looks tiny in his blocky hands that are both pivoting wildly, his elbows rising and falling, weaving the car around the road as if he's trying to dodge phantoms streaming in low toward the windshield.

I was tolerating his drifting around the two-lane road when we were on flat ground and could see a mile ahead of us. Now we're starting to drive up into the mountains and we can't see what might be around the next hairpin turn. Gina and I snap on our seat belts.

"Stay in our lane. Stay in our damned lane." I'm the one yelling now.

"You don't believe me?"

That he's the best driver in Morocco? No, of course I don't believe him. He can't possibly think he's fooling me; I can see that we're weaving all over the pavement. In fact, right now, as we approach a blind turn on this narrow mountain road he is entirely in the other lane.

I cringe, Gina cringes, he sings. We turn the corner and there is no other car in sight. He swings wide and we return to our lane.

I don't care if he knows this road. A car could have been in that lane and we would have a head-on collision on a mountain road with no guardrail. This is insane.

"I show you." He pulls his driver's credentials off its perch above the rearview mirror.

"NO. Just drive." Gina yells this time.

We're stunned by what he does next. To prove to us just how good a driver he is, he turns around and hands us his driver's credentials. He's completely pivoted at the waist, facing back toward us as the car speeds forward. He's grinning.

"What the hell are you doing? Turn around and look at the road!" I yell.

I grab the credentials out of his hand in hopes that he will now turn around and face the front.

He pivots back into his seat and talks over his shoulder.

"See the stars?"

Sure enough, there are four stars on the bottom right corner of the card. It looks official, government-issued. There is no possible way a star could mean the same thing in Morocco as it does in the States. Maybe this is four stars out of a possible ten stars—or out of one hundred. Maybe the government puts a star on the card to mark every head-on collision the driver has suffered.

We hand the card back, and he snaps it into place above the mirror. Just in time. We're approaching another turn. Once again, he's in the wrong lane, sweeps wide around the blind turn, and eases into our lane. There are no approaching cars in sight.

As we near the next blind turn, a mountain wall on our left and guardrail-less cliff on our right, I am actually starting to relax. The road was obviously empty so his drifting around wasn't adding any risk. In an hour we would be over the mountains. Perhaps there was nothing to worry about.

We were going about thirty miles an hour as we rounded the corner, entirely in the wrong lane. We all saw the oncoming truck at the same time.

Hassan jerked down his right elbow and our front left bumper took the impact, crushed flat by the full force of the truck. We began sliding across the road toward the cliff.

There wasn't a word spoken in the car as it continued its glide to the cliff edge. I don't even remember the sound of the radio, as if it too were holding its breath in anticipation of what was to come. Then friction finally took full hold and we came to a stop.

I turned right and looked out Gina's window. There was no going out that door—it was hanging over the cliff edge.

"Better go out your side," Gina observed as I swung open my door and was relieved to look down at pavement.

Her suggestion was nearly drowned out by Hassan. He had slammed his shoulder into his door, burst out of the car, and was now running up to the dump truck screaming at the top of his voice. We had just eluded death and rather than pause and exhale in relief, Hassan was a frothing bull.

We unclipped our seat belts and stepped out onto the road.

The dump truck driver had stepped down from his cab and he and Hassan were now screaming, noses nearly touching, eyes fixed on each other. Their hands were chopping at the air, the words pouring out in thick superheated streams.

We didn't intervene in that melee. Instead, Gina and I sat down on the side of the road to wait it out. Surely, at the pace they were going, they would wear out in a few minutes.

"Take a look up there," Gina said pointing up at the mountainside. "This must be Dead Man's Turn."

Dozens of rock cairns, stone memorials, were stacked on the incline rising up from the road. We weren't the first to have trouble turning this corner. No doubt, we wouldn't be the last.

The first hour of the drivers' argument went by with almost no discernible decline in intensity. Evidently, a Moroccan's well runs deep.

Not mine. I stood up and strolled to the car to bring us back some water.

I can't remember who said it first, Gina or me. Either way, we were both wondering the same thing. Hassan was entirely at fault: "What could he possibly have to scream about?"

To this day I don't know the answer to that question. Some things simply defy explanation.

If Hassan was right about one thing it was this: cars don't come down this road very often. I would guess it was another half hour before the first car arrived.

The responses of Hassan and the dump truck driver were immediate and identical. They turned, saw the car coming, and ran toward it. Inexplicably, they both began yelling at the new driver on the scene. Rather than being disturbed, the new arrival became immediately engaged, animated by the argument.

The three were now standing in a circle, the third person now creating a bit of space, broadening the battlefield. The hands that once served as axes, chopping at the air, now were more expressive, reenacting the scene for the objective third party. Hassan was clearly yelling out his version of the events, pointing back at the dump truck, then pivoting his palm parallel to the ground, sweeping it across the air mimicking the slide of his car. The dump truck driver was yelling his version at the same time, looking straight into the eyes of the new arrival.

What else could the new driver do? He wasn't going anywhere: the road was blocked by the dump truck and our car. So he started yelling also.

A second car pulled up and the three men now ran to the latest person to arrive on the scene.

A half hour later a car pulled up behind the dump truck, trying to go down the mountain. Again, the clot migrated to the new driver, pulling him in, expanding their numbers, circling, like players in a rugby scrum.

A second hour ticked by.

The end came abruptly, unexpectedly. The shouting simply stopped. The drivers dispersed and went back to their cars, the dump truck driver stepped back up into his cab.

No money was exchanged. No one took out paper and pen to write down the name of an insurance company or a license plate. It didn't end happily; there were no slaps on the back or merriment. But there was no bloodshed either, no fists thrown. It just ended.

But one thing was clear: each new driver had become engaged in the event. This wasn't about figuring out who was at fault; no one was accused in the end, no retribution paid.

It wasn't conflict resolution. But it wasn't pointless Y chromosome bluster either. It simply seemed to be an opportunity, a stimulating occasion to socialize, like women in Tanzania crowded around the community well, chatting while filling their buckets. They all wanted to experience a shared purpose.

There was a desire by all of the drivers on the road that afternoon to be part of something outside of just themselves, and this happened to be what came along. Years ago, I wouldn't have cared about any of this. Now, I confess, I understood it, and there was an undeniable appeal to it all. If I had spoken the language, I would have willingly stepped into the clash.

As Hassan started heading back to the car, we stood up.

He grabbed what was left of the quarter panel, pulled it off, and heaved it down the side of the cliff. He opened the door, sat down in his seat, and turned the key. Our car started, as did everyone else's along the road. Before driving ahead, he turned around in his seat and faced us.

He grinned back at us, beaming; he was in his element.

He was the worst driver I have ever known; that was undeniable. But I couldn't help but like him. The radio blaring, his voice once again shouting out over the music, we were back on our journey over the mountain.

On our return to the United States, we learned something remarkable.

Against all odds, Patsy Spier had persuaded key senators, Republicans and Democrats alike, to sponsor an amendment to suspend the U.S. government support for International Military Education and Training funds to the Indonesian military until the ambush had been investigated and the shooters apprehended.

She had walked the halls of Congress, and successfully pressed her case with President Bush's administration. In time, and as more evidence came in, the Bush administration recognized the value of suspending funding.

As I caught up on the events when we returned from Morocco, I found newspapers that followed Patsy's story and described whom she was meeting with. They read like a who's who of politics: she had met with the deputy secretary of defense, the director of the FBI, the president of Indonesia, and senator after senator after senator.

When the full impact of Patsy's success finally settled into my thinking, I again did something I never thought I would do. I dug through my sock drawer.

I was searching for the amulet the Lama had given me on my way up Mount Everest.

I didn't dig through the drawer out of a sense of nostalgia. I wasn't trying to recall the challenges I had faced. Instead, I was digging to get some perspective.

There, sitting in the back of the drawer, untouched since I had tossed it in, was the amulet. Beside the amulet was the scrap of paper that I had written the words on before the Sherpa had sewn the amulet up tight in the threads from a silk scarf that the Lama had blessed.

I unfolded the scrap and stared down at the letters for the first time in four years:

Why did I go back to that sock drawer?

I was no longer on the journey I had intended. Sure, I would finish my list of mountains and oceans, I wasn't about to give up on the record, but this had become about so much more than surfing and climbing. In fact, my plan had become unexpectedly complicated.

What was the likelihood that I would meet Gina on my expedition to Everest? And what was the likelihood that my life would get entwined with Patsy Spier's?

I didn't expect that the amulet would explain why these unlikely events occurred. I didn't expect the amulet to explain why my life, my attitude, was changing.

But what I knew was this: if I traced back the timeline of my surfing and climbing record to just before these improbable things started to happen, it would be that moment in the Lama's prayer room.

That's not to say he was the cause of it all. But perhaps something relevant did happen at that moment. Maybe he saw me for who I was. Perhaps he looked into my eyes, saw my character, and knew that the journey I was on would deepen me far more than I expected. The mountain would not be under my control, he knew that, and perhaps he knew I didn't fully appreciate that fact.

If the Lama did size me up at that moment, then I wanted to

know what he concluded. Somehow, that insight was contained in the amulet.

I pulled the amulet out of the drawer and hung it on our mantel over the fireplace alongside an old pair of battered crampons that had been my contact with the snow on all the peaks on my journey.

That wasn't the only change I made.

A pillar, one of those parts of my foundation that I thought I would never change, was about to fall.

One thing that made Gina completely unlike a typical Brooklyn Italian is that she had suffered frostbite. Willingly.

At the age of sixteen, Gina's mother divorced and moved her three daughters to Denver. A few times every winter, with fresh snow piling up in the mountains, Gina would skip school and go to the slopes and ski until her legs were limp and her fingers were chilled to the bone, hardened numb.

The first time we went to a slope together, in Jackson, Wyoming, she decided to be accommodating and agreed to go snowboarding with me, her first time.

After an hour of slamming down backward on the snow, deep bruises thickening on her tailbone, she pointed at the snowboard and stared back at me:

"I don't need to learn how to ride that thing. I'm here to have some fun, not bruise my ass."

There was no discussion. She had been gracious, given it a shot, but kindness has its limits. Her mind was made up. "I'm switching to skis, I'll see you in a minute."

When she returned, with skis on, we hit the black diamond runs and I spent the rest of the day going down the slope beside her. She was on skis, I was on a snowboard—we were in sync on the path, but we each chose a different method to navigate the terrain. She was self-assured, a solid partner beside me, but working it her own way. I didn't need her there, but I wanted her there.

It may have been at that moment that I had this dramatic realization: there was no reason for me to want to be apart from her.

Gina had a similar realization about me. But it wasn't that day, and the circumstances were of an entirely different sort.

A pool of saliva is forming on the hardwood of our living room floor. The dog is spread flat, the drool falling off the tongue in thick pea-sized droplets. The smell of boiled shoes hovers over its patchy mottled hair, the skin hangs on the bones like a swaddled X-ray. There is nothing appealing about this dog.

"If no one adopts her this afternoon, they'll put her down tomorrow," Gina explains.

Clearly, the dog didn't understand that her clock was counting down. If she knew that today was her last day, she'd be putting on a better show. Fetching, shaking my hand, balancing on back paws, anything to raise her prospects. Instead, she's drooling on the floor, panting, immobile, and sniffing for food, hoping, I suppose, that a slab of bacon will suddenly appear under her nose.

"Why is she drooling so much?" I knew nothing about dogs, so it seemed like a reasonable question.

"Slake, it's a hundred degrees outside and she's got a thick coat on her. She's hot."

We'd walked the dog over to our house from the Humane Society van that was parked down the street for an animal adoption event. What should have been a five-minute walk took nearly fifteen with the dog stopping every few steps to sit and pant, then lift up and struggle for a few more paces only to pause again, pee, and wheeze.

Gina knew how I felt about this. I'd been asked by a reporter once whether I had a pet and I said: "No. I don't let any living thing in my house that can't open a bottle of scotch." Gina had read that quote; she knew what she was up against.

I was unimpressed. "She can't seem to do anything but lie there."

If Gina had wanted me to take an interest in a dog, I would have expected something with more life, a bit of teeth, an occasional snarl.

"It's your decision," Gina said. "We should take her back to the van in a few minutes." Then she walked out of the room, leaving me alone with the dog.

I got down on the ground beside it and looked into its eyes.

That dog needed me if it was going to survive one more day, but that didn't matter to either of us—me or the dog. I didn't see pleading in her eyes, and I didn't feel any pity for her.

Instead, I felt something else.

This wasn't who the dog really was. The exterior—the patchy skin, the tongue draping over the teeth, the stench—was just a dismal cover. All that was the result of a hard past. There was a different dog underneath all that smear and waste.

So why not give her a chance, I thought. I could pull her back from the edge and find out who she is. I could care; I did care.

The dog stared back at me, unblinking.

I stood back up as Gina came into the room.

"Let's call her Pemba," I said.

"Why Pemba?" Gina asked.

"It's the Sherpa word for Saturday, today, the day I decided to keep her."

Within a few weeks the dog started to thicken, eventually bulking to a muscled eighty-five pounds. The patches filled in, the stench subsided, the pools of drool dried up. All of that was replaced by a steady companion that trotted by my side down the street or trail, alert for squirrels and a crumb. Eager, enthused, always ready to charge at the day the moment the door swung open, those were the genuine qualities; that is what lay underneath the weathered coat.

Gina knew the same was true of me, that something solid lay underneath my gnarled exterior. She had seen indications of something deeper in me. I had written the piece for the *Post*, I had talked to congressional staff; I could care about something outside myself. My decision to keep that ragged old dog was the last confirmation she needed. It hadn't surprised her. She told me that when she walked out of the room, she knew I was capable of accepting that dog. Pemba sealed it.

I proposed to Gina, and she accepted. Pillar #1, that determination I had to never get married, fell away. It didn't collapse with a dramatic crash of blocks and ash; it didn't leave a heap of rubble. Instead, that pillar, that certainty I thought I had, faded away without a sound, as if it had never really been there in the first place.

We made our wedding plans. As a result, in just a few months' time, I would find out exactly what the Lama had in mind when he gave me that amulet. There would be no need for speculation, no need to hunt down ancient scrolls or consult master linguists to decipher the amulet's meaning. I was going back to the source. Gina and I were heading to Nepal to get married in the Thyangboche monastery, the very spot where I had received the amulet.

I planned to have another audience with the Lama. This time when I asked him a question, I would make sure to get the answer in a language that I could understand.

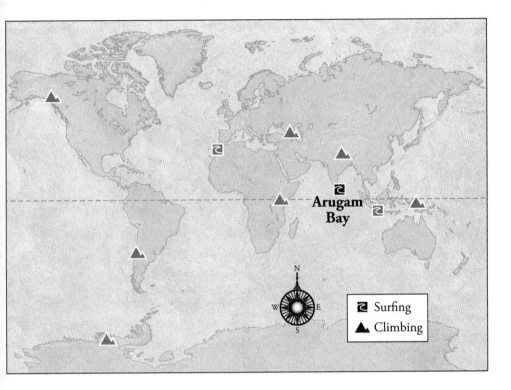

Chapter 8

INTERCONNECTED

The owner of the teahouse speaks only broken English, but if I understand her correctly, then the hat she is trying to jam into Gina's backpack is at least one hundred years old. Gina is standing beside her, protesting the offer. But the owner is determined; jaw clenched tight, she throws her shoulder into Gina and continues to force the muffin-shaped cap into the depths of the backpack.

We stopped here just a few minutes ago and while waiting for some tea the owner asked us what we were doing in Namche Bazaar.

"We're on our way to the Thyangboche monastery to get married."

Her squeal required no translation. It was evident that she was delighted for us. Then she got inquisitive.

"Where are wedding clothes?"

"We're wearing them," Gina explained.

Personally, I thought our wedding attire was stunning. I had on a pair of lightweight gray Asolo GTX hiking boots that had just a touch of marsh-green shading, complemented by a deep-black North Face zip-up all-weather Gore-Tex jacket. Gina's mauve Marmot PreCip jacket added a touch of color to the occasion without being overstated. In the event of a chill, she had a pair of Outdoor Research mitts with removable fleece liners—a beautiful accessory piece.

Evidently, the teahouse owner saw things differently. She snorted.

"You will wear my wedding clothes." She turned and left the room.

This woman was a complete stranger; we had known her for all of two minutes.

She returned moments later with several pieces of clothing, neatly folded, stacked in her arms. On the top of that stack was a dead squirrel.

"I married in this. Mother married in this. Her mother married in this. You will marry in this."

She walks over to Gina's backpack, unclips the top, and starts shoving in pieces from the stack.

"No, please, no. That is too generous. Too kind. I can't accept." Gina leaps up to stop the woman from mashing her family tradition into the backpack.

Several things are going through my mind at that moment. First is this: when will the tea be ready? Second, I realize that this moment typifies a difference between our two countries, Nepal and the United States.

Interconnected

Imagine driving to your wedding and you pass through a small town and stop at the local diner for a cup of coffee. You don't know the owner, but when you tell her you're on your way to get married she hands you her one-hundred-year-old wedding gown. That would be shocking in the United States, but it is entirely unsurprising here in this Buddhist village of a few hundred shacks dotting a foothill of the Himalayas.

There is one thing that does surprise me: that dead squirrel on top of the stack of clothes. I get up off my stool to get a closer look. I have no intention of inserting myself into the shoving match; the teahouse owner has the instincts of an NBA forward, shouldering back against the defender, pressing in to get the score. If I get too close she might elbow me in the teeth.

I look past her arm at the hide in her right hand. It's not a squirrel. It's a yak skin hat, the hair thick, long, and tangled. If Gina were wearing this in Wyoming during hunting season, she'd be shot on sight, mistaken as a wandering buffalo.

Despite Gina's protests, we all know that there is only one way this can end. Gina accepts the clothes. "Thank you so much. This is just amazing."

"Drop off on your way back," is the woman's final instruction before pouring our tea.

Namche Bazaar is the doorway to the Himalayas, the last village before the terrain begins its sharp rise up into the mountains. Every Saturday merchants from across the Khumbu Valley in Nepal come here to trade their goods. Those market days are a centuries-old tradition and they still draw traders from Tibet, who cross over the high mountain passes. As a result of this being a trading post, the villagers are used to seeing people pass through with packs to be emptied or filled with goods.

Gina's pack is now stuffed with a traditional Sherpa wedding outfit. With that, we continue on up the trail toward the Thyangboche monastery.

The monastery shows no sign of change from the way it looked years before, when we first passed through, me on my way to climb Everest, Gina on the trek. It remains remote and solitary. Those qualities carry both advantages and disadvantages.

On the upside, there are no crowds to manage at the wedding, no parking headaches, no band to book, no dilemmas over who sits at which table. We invited friends and family to join us and a few have come. The rest are waiting back at home to throw us a party on our return.

The downside is that the monks here have no idea that we are coming. There was no way to communicate with them; there are no phone lines here or electric grid to power a connection to the Internet. They wouldn't have a wedding ceremony planned and ready, but I thought that was a manageable problem for a simple reason. The monks live in a daily cycle of prayer and fasting. With our arrival, they would have a welcome break from the routine. I assumed they could whip up a ceremony in short order. And so they did. So did the owner of the teahouse near the monastery. When I explained to him why we were here, he had an immediate question for us.

"Where are you wedding clothes?"

Gina explained what happened in Namche and he smiled, admiring the clothes as Gina pulled them out of her backpack. He nodded approvingly at the massive yak skin hat.

"You?" he said staring at me.

I explained that I planned to wear what I had on. Once again, a teahouse owner failed to see the flair in my wedding attire of boots and all-weather jacket.

"You will wear my wedding clothes," and he went into a back room.

Interconnected

There is a rustic charm to the Sherpa's wedding cloak. The hat, however, is an embarrassment. It's at least three sizes too small for me. It looks like I'm balancing a teacup on my head; it would slide off if I made any quick movements. The owner beamed with pride, so I accepted his offer to wear his cloak. I respectfully clasped the hat in my hands behind my back for the duration.

The monks went deep into their closets in arranging our ceremony. We could hear the drums and chimes as we walked up the steps of the monastery the next morning and passed, as we had done years earlier, that block of stone that they believe carries the impression of the Buddha's feet.

The assembly hall was packed full, monks sitting shoulder to shoulder, their chant a soft resonant murmur that filled the room. Along the side wall were several saffron-colored cushions, laid out spaciously for us. Beside them sat three monks, each with a seven-foot-long narrow horn, the mouthpiece in their hands, the neck stretching out far in front of them with the end flaring to a wide opening that rested on a wooden block.

The chanting is rhythmic, seductive, and so alluring that some monks will never get outside its range. There are monks at the Thyangboche monastery who have never known a larger world. Dropped off by their parents when they were just a few years old, their days are spent walking only between the assembly hall and a wooden cot in their small stone shelter.

The chant would occasionally crescendo and then all the instruments would break in at once, the horn blaring out over the sound of the drums and chime.

Then, suddenly, all went silent.

Two monks escorted us to the front of the hall, to a raised platform. There, his head respectfully bowed, sat the monk who was leading the ceremony. It was at that point that we literally tied the knot. We lowered our heads and the monk took two red strings out of the pocket in his cloak and tied one around each of our necks. Gina and I turned and faced each other, touched foreheads—that was all the contact that was allowed in the assembly hall—and the ceremony was complete.

Up to this point, I had no opportunity to look the head monk in the eyes. As we were turning to leave the assembly hall I glanced back at him. Staring back at me was an entirely unfamiliar face. This was not the Lama who had given me the amulet.

On occasion, a Lama will choose to withdraw for a period of seclusion. This can last a few weeks, or it can last for years. The Most Holy Rinpoche of the Khumbu, the Lama who had given me the amulet, was in seclusion and the monks expected that it might be months before he would emerge from his quarters and resume contact with the monastery. He had decided to go into seclusion just three days before our arrival. If I were superstitious, I would have thought he was avoiding me.

While the Lama was in seclusion, the monastery had a caretaker monk. He was not regarded as a reincarnate; he would not be offering audiences to travelers or dispensing wisdom. He was simply charged with managing affairs until the Lama reemerged.

And so, the amulet would, once again, defy translation. But we were now traveling on into Tibet and surely, I thought, someone there could translate the amulet.

There are two generic routes up Everest. You can climb it from the south side, the Nepali side, as I did. Or, you can climb it from the north side, the Tibetan side, as did the Russian I met on the summit. I had never seen the summit of Everest from the Tibetan side until now. We are staring up at it, near the town of Tingri, Tibet.

Years ago, when I was planning the climb I had to make a decision about which side to climb from. If you climb Everest from the Tibetan side the logistics are easy. You don't have the two-week-long trek to Base Camp accompanied by a team of yaks hauling a ton of gear and supplies that is required on the Nepali side. Instead, on the Tibetan side, you can drive to Base Camp. Despite that advantage to the Tibetan side approach, when I discussed it with Jim Williams we opted for the Nepali side.

"If you climb from the north, you drive in and miss the culture," Jim had said.

If we had climbed the Tibetan side I would have had an entirely different experience, an entirely different life. That obvious fact was made all the more apparent as I stared up at Everest that afternoon, with Gina at my side.

The next few weeks were filled with visits to monasteries, sanctuaries, a school for Buddhist monks who memorize scroll after scroll and train in the art of debate. We covered nearly a thousand miles in a jeep, penetrating deep into the heart of Buddhist territory, once joining a group of more than a hundred monks in their circumambulations of ancient temples. You would think that with all those miles we covered we would find someone who could translate the amulet. But no, we didn't find anyone.

There were other, perhaps more reliable ways than scouring monasteries. When we returned to the States I would find a scholar, someone who had dedicated years to deciphering ancient Buddhist scrolls, and I would ask him what it meant.

I still had options; but for the first time I remember having this thought: perhaps the amulet will never be translated.

Getting into Tibet was easier than getting out.

We had initially hopped a bus to get into Tibet from Kathmandu,

Nepal. We didn't have a return ticket, since we didn't want to have a set return date. Instead, we had the name and address of a fixer in Lhasa, Tibet, who could help us get out.

The address was to a warehouse complex just outside the town center. When we pushed open the door to the second floor, we realized that this wasn't the den of a stealthy deal maker who gently contacts the right authorities to assist an occasional traveler. This was an industrial-scale operation. The room had about thirty Chinese in it, sitting at desks, working phones, fans whirring.

We called out the name on our slip of paper and got a shout from a nearby desk.

"We need two tickets out of Lhasa to Kathmandu," we explained.

The Fixer looked back at us, silent.

We told him who we got his contact information from, hoping that he would recognize his friend's name and then pick up his phone and start dialing madly, just as everyone else in the room appeared to be doing.

He didn't pick up the phone. Instead he simply said: "No tickets."

"When will tickets be available?" I asked.

"Not this week, next week. I will let you know."

We gave him our hotel address. There was no problem with waiting a week; that would give us the time to visit a place I had been curious about: Lake Namtso, located deep in the Tibetan Plateau.

The Tibetan Plateau is one of the harshest environments on the planet, perhaps second only to Antarctica. A major difference between the two is that people actually choose to live their entire lives on the plateau.

The plateau is vast, four times the size of Texas, and it sits at an average elevation of fifteen thousand feet. Surrounded by a sanctuary of peaks, the only way to enter the plateau is by going over a mountain pass, the lowest point of which is nearly eighteen thousand feet.

The weather is severe: the average daily temperature hovers around zero degrees and drops to forty below in the wintertime. The people who live here are unique in the world, one of the last of the nomadic people who make their livelihood by driving their livestock across grasslands. The yak is the core of their existence. They eat the meat, make clothes out of the hides, carve prayers into the horns and scatter them along the plateau. They go over the mountain passes to trade the hides in exchange for other goods. The lifestyle seems timeless, unchanged for centuries.

On the southeastern corner of the expansive plateau is the saltwater lake of Namtso, our destination. It too delivers a sense of deep time.

As Gina and I stroll along the sandy lake edge, my boots suddenly make a crunching sound, like I'm walking on cornflakes. I look down and find sea shells. We are standing at a point more than one thousand miles away from the nearest ocean, yet here, at my feet, are shells. Those shells had been lying there for eons, the remnants of the unfortunate ocean life that got trapped here when the continents collided more than 300 million years ago.

This place is time's mirror. Every shell is a story, the home of an ancient sea creature carried forward in time millions of years. The grains of sand tell the tale of an ocean floor, lifted up tens of thousands of feet in a clash of landmasses. The surrounding mountains are the vanguard, the leading edge of that violent continental surge, finally reined in, slowed, by gravity itself.

Here we stood, one moment, one drop in time, connected to an entire stream of history. We were part of earth's story in a way I had never experienced before, not while I was on the top of any summit, not even when I was on the highest point on earth looking down.

Staring at a shell in the palm of my hand, I felt time. I don't mean I felt my age. And I don't mean time as in the "t" of a physics equation. I mean the past, made present. I experienced time, its expanse and roil, the grand sweep of it all.

I put the shell in my pocket. It would eventually find its place on the mantel, beside the amulet.

———

"You don't need ticket," the Fixer is explaining six days later.

He is insistent, confident.

"Go to airport tomorrow morning, you will get on."

"How will they let us board without a ticket, no boarding pass, no exit stamp, nothing?" I asked.

"It is all arranged."

Either this guy was extraordinarily good at rigging the system, or we were being conned. His delivery was comfortable, not a hint of exaggeration, no indication that he was spinning a tale. We took him at his word and paid.

When we arrived at the airport the next morning there was a crowd of people; more than I would think could fit on a single plane. The majority of them seemed to be from a tour group. Unlike us, their flight plans would have been worked out months ago, confirmed by travel agents and perhaps double-checked or triple-checked by the anxious traveler. We weren't in the habit of traveling in arranged groups and so instead we stood off to the side, apart from the thick tourist sea; we were ticketless and wary.

When our moment came, it was hyperefficient. An airline employee walked up to us, picking us out of the crowd.

He said something like: "Sakey? Elito?"

That was close enough to Francis Slakey and Gina Eppolito.

"Yes," we both responded.

He waved his hand for us to follow him and we walked past the crowd and onto the plane. No ticket ever exchanged hands, just as the Fixer had promised. He pointed us to a couple of seats near the front and then turned and walked off the plane.

On our return to the U.S., Gina and I exchanged wedding rings. She had worked with a local jeweler and designed a ring for me that expressed a few key aspects of our relationship. The ring consists of two separate bands of metal; they are bound together, but able to move independently. The ring is heavy; Gina knew that our getting married was a big decision, not to be taken lightly. And there is one last, practical touch to the design. The inside of the ring doesn't contain an inscription; there are no words, no date. Instead, the inside is filled with dozens of metal bumps—a recognition and acceptance of what two independent people are sure to face.

In the summer of 2006, we returned to Asia. There was something there I had to finish. I needed to surf the Indian Ocean and I wanted it to be somewhere interesting. I picked Sri Lanka. The beach I had in mind wouldn't be easy to get to, but it would allow me to check one more box on the To Do List. But first, along the way, we would visit Bhutan because we had both been curious about the reclusive kingdom for years.

Bhutan is one of the most isolated countries in the world. On a beachball-sized globe, the country is smaller than a penny. To the rest of the world, that's about all it's worth.

Bhutan has no significant natural resources: no valuable ores, no oil, no precious mineral deposits. Tucked deep in the Himalayas and sandwiched between Tibet and India, it is also one of the most mountainous countries in the world. A few paved roads link the largest towns; dirt roads fan out to some of the villages. But it is the narrow footpaths that switchback along the steep mountainsides and connect remote villages that are the real thoroughfares of Bhutan.

As a result of all this, Bhutan has been completely ignored by history. It has never been invaded, occupied, colonized, or exploited. The great sweep of history that shaped Asia—Alexander the Great, Genghis Khan, the Chinese dynasties, the British, the Soviets—all of them bypassed the Kingdom of Bhutan.

Bhutan may not have had anything to offer the world, but it did take one thing from it. Fifteen hundred years ago, it imported something that forever after shaped its development: Buddhism. And for the most part, it rejected everything else. Even now, it has limited access to television, Internet, movies, and world news. To preserve their identity, to minimize the intrusion of the materialism that Buddhism rejects, all outside influences, Western culture in particular, are kept at arm's length. Tourists can only travel on one of a few government-approved routes; no straying allowed. To ensure close monitoring of every tourist, the government tightly caps the number of travel visas it issues each year.

I understood the reasons for the restrictions. I appreciated their interest in preserving their identity. I just didn't want to be restricted to only moving along the official route; that wasn't the way Gina and I traveled. But a colleague of mine put us in touch with one of the few Americans, a teacher, who had traveled freely in Bhutan and had been allowed to stay.

I contacted the teacher; he was living in the States again, and we talked it over. While he was living in Bhutan he had gotten to know someone who was well connected in the ministry of tourism. His name was Kencho Thukten. He gave me Kencho's e-mail address and wished me luck.

It is remarkable, the lines that connect people. You can strike up a conversation with someone, a stranger even, and discover that you have a friend in common, that your aunts were from the same town, or that his best friend can grease your way into Bhutan. It seems on those occasions that we are all like strands of DNA, spun around each other in a double helix.

I sent an e-mail to Kencho saying that Gina and I were interested in traveling to Bhutan but that we would only come if we could do a bit of roaming. I asked him if he could help arrange it.

About a week later, I received the briefest of e-mails: "What would you like to do in my country?"

This seemed like a completely wide-open offer, not restricted to the Bhutanese government's preapproved travel routes. It was an opportunity for us to be creative.

We wanted to come up with something unique, something that would allow us to experience whatever it is that defines Bhutan. It seemed to me that Bhutan's core qualities, the aspects that have shaped and guided it for more than a millennium, are Buddhism and its noncommercialism.

There was a book published several years ago titled *Material World: A Global Family Portrait*. Photographers were dispatched to countries across the globe and asked to take a photo of the typical local family with all their goods spread out in front of them. Two photos are on the cover of the book: on top is a picture of the typical smiling American family, and below it is a picture of the typical Bhutanese family. The American family's possessions are familiar and numerous. Couches, televisions, desks, beds, cabinets are all arranged wide across the photo, filling the cul-de-sac in front of their Texas home with a two-car garage.

The photo of the Bhutanese family couldn't be more different. Mountains rise behind their small stone house and they stare up at the photographer with firm unsmiling faces. The father and mother and two small children wear traditional wraps, one of the older sons wears the robes of a monk. A few farming tools are stuck into the ground behind them and in the foreground they have the sum of their possessions: a few bowls and blankets, some candles, a lamp.

This wasn't a photo of the disadvantaged, the poor and suffering of Bhutan. From the things I had read, the people I had spoken with, I had learned that this was a remarkably happy nation. Underlying that happiness, I was told, was Buddhist philosophy.

"You have to see if for yourself," the American teacher who'd given me Kencho's e-mail address had said. "All that talk of nonmaterialism— it's for real. You've got to experience the Buddhism there to believe it."

That, I decided, is what I wanted to get out of a trip to Bhutan. I could think of only one way to make that happen. I typed the message out on my computer screen at work and read it back to Gina over the phone: "We would like to learn about Buddhism from one of your Lamas."

It was simple, straightforward. It was also practical in a way I hoped Kencho would appreciate. After all, you go to Italy and you drink wine, you go to Bhutan and you take in a little Buddhism.

Plus, there might be a bonus here. I was getting nowhere decoding the amulet, perhaps if I absorbed some of the philosophy behind it I could make some progress.

"Let's see what happens," Gina said. I pushed the send button.

A couple weeks passed and I thought nothing would come of it. Then a reply arrived from Kencho: the Lama will meet with you. However, he is in a small village. No tourists have ever been there and there is no hotel. You will have to stay with a local family. Is this okay?

Okay? It was perfect.

———

"We must make it to the turn by four o'clock or we will have to wait two hours," Kencho says, a touch of urgency in his voice, as we drive down the one main road in Bhutan on our way to meet Lama Kinle.

"What happens at four?"

"The road closes to move the dirt."

"And why are they moving dirt?"

"So we do not anger the Snake Goddess," Kencho replied.

That answer made perfect sense to him. Gina and I needed more information.

A few months earlier, the government had decided they wanted to widen the road we were on, and they went about blasting and paving their way down the street, trucks moving steadily forward in a caravan, tar getting laid. Then they got to the mountain turn we were approaching, planning to blast the rock out with explosives. The people who live in the area warned that a goddess lives in the trees just above the turn and that the workers should forgo widening the road. The locals were ignored and the charges were set. Just before the explosives were detonated, one of the workers fell off the cliffside.

The locals cautioned the government that the goddess was upset and that the worker's death was an omen. The government appreciated the warning, and respectfully suspended activity for a few days, then they resumed their plan. Charges were placed, and again a worker fell to his death.

That, evidently, was proof enough. The government decided that rather than blasting the rock, which clearly upset the goddess, they would instead fill dirt into the ravine below and run the road straight across to the other side. The job would now take an estimated six months, rather than the two days it would have taken to blast out the rock.

That decision would never happen in the Western world, but the Bhutanese government isn't like any institution in the Western world. They don't address these issues by consulting a technical specialist. Instead, they consult a Lama. And it was the Lama, not an engineer or transportation expert, who had advised that the government immediately cease the blasting and instead fill the ravine with dirt.

We didn't make it to the turn by four o'clock, so we pulled the car to a stop and watched the dump trucks go by.

To pass the time, I thought we'd take a look at the project. I was curious just how much extra work the government had made for itself by opting to fill in the ravine.

When I looked over the cliff edge I was astounded. The ravine looked to be one hundred feet deep. Filling this in would require thousands and thousands of loads of dirt, like filling a bathtub one thimbleful at a time. Equally surprising was that the curve in the road was modest and all this could have been so easily handled with one simple blasting of the rock. They had created hundreds, perhaps thousands, of times more work for themselves.

"I can't believe this," I said shaking my head.

"Why?" asked Kencho.

"All this extra work because they think there's a goddess?"

"Snake Goddess, yes," Kencho replied, oblivious to my disbelief.

"Would you like to see her?" he asked.

He was serious. The road wouldn't open for another hour, he explained, and since we were in no hurry, he would be happy to take us up the cliff to see the goddess.

I stared at Gina, trying to make sense of this.

"Let me get my camera." Gina ran back to the car for her photo gear.

There was no path up the cliffside so we had to climb cautiously, slowly, giving Kencho time to explain what he considered to be a few key points.

"The goddess can manifest herself in many forms. She has chosen to manifest as a snake. This is very powerful."

We topped out on a ledge and he pointed to indicate that we needed to walk toward a large flat rock the size of a dinner table.

"That is where she lives. Under that rock."

He called us in for a huddle when we were just a few steps away from the rock.

"You must be very careful. Show respect. Do not upset the goddess."

Never having met a goddess before, I had no idea how to show respect.

"I will go first," Kencho offered, sensing my uncertainty.

He crept forward a few feet and, reverently I suppose, peeked under the rock.

I knew how this would unfold. He would come back and tell us that the goddess was gone, out for an early dinner or some such thing. Nothing was there, nothing could be there, and he would provide an excuse.

He quietly got up and walked back to us.

"She is there."

That was unexpected. "Okay, then. Let's go see a goddess," Gina said.

She and I walked together up to the stone, bent over, and peered in.

Just a few inches away from us, uncoiled and indifferent, was one of the smallest snakes I have ever seen. It was about a quarter inch thick, maybe eight inches long at the most.

We stood up and looked back at Kencho.

"This little snake, is that the goddess?" I asked. Maybe this was a newborn and the goddess was nearby, thick and threatening, hunting for some food.

"Yes. Show respect."

I showed respect by not bursting out laughing. As Gina snapped a couple pictures, I looked over the edge and down at the ravine. For the next half year dump trucks would be driving up to the edge, unloading dirt, filling in the hole inch by inch. All this because of a snake no bigger than a pencil.

"Gina, take a picture of the ravine, would you? No one is going to believe this story."

"We are in a world of darkness, and people are sleeping through it," Lama Kinle intones.

The words come slowly, thoughtfully. He isn't reciting from a book; he is carefully formulating his thoughts. He has never met with Westerners before and he wants to make sure that he conveys his philosophy accurately.

He pauses, picks up a bowl, and spits in the juicy residue of the betel nut that he is chewing. As Kencho translates the words, the Lama looks back up at us and nods, smiling.

He's a fiend for the nut. At least twice over the last two hours he's reached into the pocket of his robes to remove his kit. He unscrews a small tin, picks out a betel nut, then extracts a bright green leaf. He drops the nut into the leaf, wads it up, and then pops it into his mouth. All that chewing has stained his teeth a deep shade of red.

We arrived in Dhorika the night before. The town is just a few miles from the border of Tibet, deep in the Himalayas. There is no electricity, no running water. We are the first Westerners to come here and we are a marvel to this farming village of about twenty houses and a hundred inquisitive eyes.

The Bhutanese have welcomed us like family, despite the fact that we couldn't be more different. I'm an average height in America, but here, at just over six feet, I tower above the locals. Gina loves it; for the first time she is in a world where even the tallest people are at her eye level.

In this first discussion with the Lama, he is laying out some of the basics.

First, Buddhism is not a religion. The easiest way to demonstrate its nonreligious quality is to contrast it to Christianity's Lord's Prayer:

Lord's Prayer	Buddhism
Our Father	does not promote a God, Buddha was a man
Who art in Heaven	does not propose a heaven or a hell
Hallowed be Thy Name	there is no supplication
Thy Kingdom come	there is no Armageddon
Thy will be done . . .	there is no plan for the universe

An immediate question, then, is: if Buddhism doesn't promote a God, then why do the Bhutanese believe in a Snake Goddess?

Kinle explains that while Buddhism doesn't promote a God, it doesn't disallow one. It doesn't propose a heaven or a hell, but you are free to believe in them. There is no Judgment Day, but you can count down to one if you so choose.

As a result, Buddhism can be pasted on top of any manner of religious belief. And it has been, particularly here in Bhutan. There is the Snake Goddess, of course. But there's more. In the village of Dhorika, where we are staying, we've seen small shrines in the villagers' homes honoring a Tree God and a Wind God.

So if it isn't a religion, then what is it? At its core, Buddhism is a code of conduct, a path toward disciplined thinking and right action. And that, if I can ignore the pain in my back from sitting in a half lotus position for two hours, is what Lama Kinle is trying to get us to understand.

"Suffering comes from a preoccupation with yourself; happiness comes from thinking about others," Kinle explains. A root cause of disappointment in life, he clarifies, is desire. The desire for material goods gets the Lama's ire up. He urges us to master our desires, not give in to the interest in acquiring more and more goods. "Such craving will never be satisfied."

He is not delivering a disinterested lecture. Inexplicably he seems to have taken a personal interest in us. As the words are translated he always nods, and smiles, encouraging us on to the next insight.

There is also an urgency, an insistence. He wants us to—he seems to need us to—take his philosophy to heart. He behaves as if he knows us, understands our lives, and is aware of precisely how we must behave to avoid some calamity in the future.

Simplicity, generosity, compassion, these are at the core of right conduct. He sums up the day's lessons with this: "Work for the benefit of others."

On the second day, two monks again lead us to the monastery's inner sanctum, the Lama's personal prayer room. As before, Kinle sits in lotus position on a cushion, the rising sun sending shafts of light through slits in the wooden shutters.

Today, he says, we will focus on the need for clear thinking, for reasoned action. "Do not believe because it is written in a book. Do not believe because it has been handed down for generations. If after observation and analysis, if it agrees with reason and can benefit one and all, then accept it and live up to it."

He goes on to explain the fundamentals of effective meditation. I had always thought of meditation as an emptying of the mind. Perhaps for some people, that is precisely what it is. But not for Kinle. He describes his meditation as an active process, deep rhythmic breaths setting the pace, the mind then syncing up and carrying out reflection. He describes the colors he sees and sounds that he hears while meditating. His senses are attentive. He doesn't try to withdraw his body into a sensory deprivation tank.

As he nears the end of the day, he warns us of possible "shadows." Because of the need to translate, he worries that phrases may be misinterpreted, that nuances will be lost. Or, perhaps, we will mistakenly try to reinterpret things to match our own needs or points of view and the true lesson will be lost, the critical point hidden from view, masked by a shadow.

"Do you understand his concern about the shadows?" Kencho asks.

"Yes." Gina and I both nod.

"Then there is one more point he wants to make today and we must be absolutely sure that there are no shadows. You must understand it clearly."

We are riveted as the Lama whispers the final thought of the day into Kencho's ear. Kencho nods at the Lama, turns back to us, and provides this translation: "If you get to the end of your life and you have regrets that you could have done better, then you blew it."

On our final afternoon with Kinle, he clarifies who he isn't: "I am not a reincarnate Lama."

However, he explains, he does have "lineage." By that he means he knows who his teacher was, and the teacher before him, and before him, and so on. His lineage is documented on scrolls and, he says, he can trace his back to Vajradhara.

I ask Kencho to write the name down in the journal I've been keeping. Weeks later, when we've left the country and I get access to a computer, I search the name to see if there is any listing. I find that Vajradhara is the name given to the enlightened Buddha, the ordinary man who achieved the ultimate Buddhist state of mind: personal desirelessness.

It may sound boastful that Kinle claimed to trace his lineage back to the Buddha. It might seem hypocritical given that for three days he'd been recommending humility as a path to right action. But this was no boast, just the reverse. He wanted to make it clear to us that he had not achieved enlightenment and that his own views would therefore be limited. The insights he was delivering were the wisdom of others, others who have listened and reflected and passed them along for the last 2,500 years.

With that final point made, his source of insights clarified, we stand up out of the knee-numbing half lotus position and shake out our legs.

We had experienced Bhutan in precisely the way I had hoped. The village had welcomed us. The Lama had patiently spoken to us, answering every question. He gave us three days of his time and then would work late into the night to complete the necessary chores of the monastery. And, most importantly, somehow, we had bypassed the government restriction on travel and come to this remote village that Westerners had never even seen before.

"Lama Kinle, thank you so much," Gina said bowing with respect, speaking for the both of us.

Kinle laughed as if it were a joke. Then he and Kencho exchanged more whispers.

"Of course, he wishes to thank you," Kencho explained as Kinle grinned broadly.

"Why would he thank us?"

Kencho looked shocked, genuinely surprised. The Lama noticed the expression and the two exchanged more words. Kencho then turned to us with a question of his own.

"Don't you know?" Kencho asked.

"Know what?" I responded.

"The vision. The Lama had a vision the day you contacted me."

A vision?

Interconnected

"You were his parents in his former life," explained Kencho.

I was too baffled to respond. Once again, an unlikely event in my life had occurred halfway around the world. And this time, it presented a head-on collision with my worldview.

"So we aren't just married in this life," Gina said, smiling at me. "He says we were married in a past life. Sounds like destiny to me."

So much of what Kinle said had resonated with me. I could relate to his comments on nonmaterialism: I didn't have a BlackBerry, I was nearly thirty before I had a television, my closet was spare.

I appreciated the meditative path that he preached, a path away from my own self-absorption. But now, with his final words, he had dropped the r-bomb: reincarnation.

I had my fill of reincarnation on the ridgeline of Everest, while staring down at Ang Nima. Now it was back. But unlike Everest where it presented a problem, here it presented an opportunity.

The reason we were welcomed to Bhutan, allowed to travel to this remote village where Westerners had never been, and spend three days in personal audience with the Lama was because he thought I was his father and Gina his mother in his previous life.

The Lama's belief had brought me here, and I welcomed that. I had no reason to complain or criticize, only thank him.

He never had the opportunity to immerse himself in science the way I had, but he had the same desire to explain his world and he was doing it in the only way he knew how, in a way that provided comfort, explanation, and meaning. I couldn't fault that. Even if I couldn't accept his beliefs, I could tolerate them.

Perhaps, I even envied them. I envied the beliefs of a man who preached desirelessness.

That's right: envy. His narrative of the world was filled with texture and warmth and humor; my scientific worldview was a sterile narrative, often reduced to colorless noninteracting components. But that view of mine was about to undergo a change, starting on a rooftop in Delhi.

There are moments when curiosity gets the better of scientists, and that can be when they produce the best work of their lives. In one case, a group of scientists decided to train the eye of the Hubble Space Telescope on an empty region of space. The region they focused on was devoid of anything known to man; it was simply an empty black void. They did it because they were curious, and the influential scientists who could make it happen were tolerant. Still, it seemed like an utter waste of time—what could be learned from looking at nothing?

For ten straight days the telescope stared intently at that blank region of space, despite the criticisms of scientists who wanted to use the scope for productive purposes. On that last day, the astronomers ended the experiment and processed the photograph. What they saw emerge in that frame was astounding, one of the single most revealing photographs ever taken.

Rather than a stark black frame, the photograph instead revealed galaxies, tens of thousands of them, where none had been expected. And each of those galaxies in turn had perhaps tens of thousands of solar systems each filled with its own sun, planets, and atmospheres. It was a startling revelation; there was more out there in the universe than scientists had ever imagined.

Any belief that our solar system occupied a unique place in the universe was shattered the moment that frame came into focus. Reveling in the discovery, the astronomers gave the photograph a wonderfully appropriate name: Deep Field.

I felt that revelatory moment myself. I felt it the day we left Bhutan and arrived in Delhi.

I had been to Delhi before, but I had never seen it the way I did that day, a result, I believe, of the newfound perspective Lama Kinle had inspired in me. When I stood on the rooftop of a hotel we'd stayed in a half dozen times before in Paharganj, overlooking Old Delhi, I saw the human equivalent of Deep Field. So much became visible.

It was a wonderful rush on my senses. The sky was speckled purple and red with kites; the air filled with the aroma of curry. As the women walked along the streets their saris created vibrant streams of blue and orange. The merchants, shoulder to shoulder, peddled cloth, juice, a haircut. I felt the press and shuffle of the city even though I stood six floors above it.

Every square foot of the scene was alive with activity—no darkness, no voids. This wasn't a sterile frame of noninteracting parts; this was vibrant, luminous humanity. I was immersed in the human Deep Field.

That is the full richness of the world. I could finally see it.

Our flight to Colombo, the former capital of the island nation of Sri Lanka, had a suspiciously light load. We've come here from Delhi so that I can surf in Arugam Bay and tick off another box on the To Do List.

As we walked down the aisle to our seats, I did a head count. There were a couple hundred seats; most of them were empty.

"There are only about twenty people on this plane," I said to Gina.

"There's no way they're making money on this. They could have canceled this flight and rolled us onto the next one. Something's not right." Her words were prophetic.

Gina was a flight attendant for American Airlines and a perk is that for years we had been flying around the world at a discount. Our plans would always be loose, hopping available flights at the last minute, not always where we intended but always heading in the right direction.

Being nonrevenue fliers, we were always the last to board, typically taking the two remaining seats on a crowded flight. Not this time.

We had anticipated that this would be a packed flight, but we walked up to the gate a half hour before the flight and they had given us seats on the spot. No one was flying to Sri Lanka. When the plane landed, we learned why. Once again, we would be navigating a country that had local insurgents battling for autonomy.

The Liberation Tigers of Tamil Eelam, or Tamil Tigers, were a militia group formed in 1976 with the goal of establishing an independent state in the northeast region of Sri Lanka. Outnumbered and outgunned by the Sri Lanka military, they created a bloody tactic that has now become the signature attack of terrorist organizations around the globe: the suicide bomber. The Tamil Tigers developed vests packed with explosives, nails, screws, bearings, and bolts. Armed with a handheld detonator, the Tamil Tigers used the suicide vests with gruesome and destructive effect across Sri Lanka for decades.

When we had planned the trip out here, the conflict had subsided and a peace process was under way. The process was an effort in balancing the autonomy demands of the Tamil ethnic minority against the desire of the governing majority Sinhalese to have the guerrilla troops disarm.

Of course, there were other places I could have chosen to surf the Indian Ocean. But A-Bay has a reputation for excellent and reliable waves and the guerrilla situation seemed manageable. The civil war was being waged hundreds of miles north of A-Bay, safely distant. The peace process had produced a lull in conflict. Those were plenty of good reasons to pick Sri Lanka.

When our plane landed in Colombo we learned that the peace process had collapsed.

A few days earlier, the Tamil Tigers had bombed a fuel depot at the airport. The government was now saying it would abandon the peace effort and engage in full-scale war to defeat the Tamil Tigers. Being unplugged from the news for weeks, we had no idea any of this was going on. Until now. As we exited the plane, airport security began shutting down the lights on the landing strip.

I walked up to a military officer who was standing nearby. "Why is the airport shutting down so early?"

"We can't guard the sky at night," he explained. "Welcome to Sri Lanka."

The officer also cautioned us that the conflict had spread to the southeastern part of the country. The Tamil Tigers had taken control of Arugam Bay.

He warned us: "You must not go there."

There is a perfectly sound decision that someone in our shoes might make at this point: turn around and go home. I risked repeating the same sort of guerrilla soldier confrontation that occurred in Indonesia, at the Freeport-McMoRan mine. Having dodged that bullet, perhaps I shouldn't press my luck and head, once again, into harm's way.

We decided otherwise. By our own choice, we were venturing onto the field of combat in a civil war. Our thinking was this: over the course of the twenty-year civil war in Sri Lanka, the Tamil Tigers had exclusively targeted government and military instillations. Civilians were not primary targets and there was no history of kidnapping or threatening foreigners. We didn't feel threatened; the risks appeared modest. We would go to A-Bay, cautiously, and with our eyes wide open.

Despite the resurgent military conflict, we found a driver willing to take us from Colombo on the western coast of the island, over the central mountains, and on to the eastern-side beach of Arugam. In distance, the trip was short, less than two hundred miles. The roads, however, are underdeveloped and slow-going. Still, we could finish the trip in a day, so long as it didn't rain and slow down the driving.

At 4 P.M., the rain started.

We had left Colombo in mid-morning and by 6 P.M. we were only halfway across the island, creeping along as the wipers swept the pounding rain off the windshield. We approached the town of Haputale and the driver pulled off the road and turned back to look at us. He was concerned, apologetic.

"I'm Sinhalese," he explained, "and I could be killed if I drive at night into Tamil areas."

He proposed two options. He could drop us off in this village; or we could wise up, drive back to Colombo with him, and forget about going to A-Bay. He urged option two. Gina and I didn't even have to talk it over. We stepped out of the car and into the pouring rain.

After knocking on a few doors, we were directed to the home of Mr. Jayasinghe, who rents out rooms to travelers. There was no answer when we knocked—that wasn't surprising since he probably never expected that anyone would be out looking for a room in the pouring rain. We pushed open the door and walked into the modest hotel. Jayasinghe appeared from around the corner the moment we called out his name.

There were five rooms and five vacancies, he explained.

That was eerie. It was a disturbingly familiar scene: rainstorm, remote hotel, too many vacancies. In Hitchcock's *Psycho,* the very first words out of Norman Bates's mouth are: "Twelve rooms, twelve vacancies."

But all that was certainly a coincidence. Our circumstances might be similar to the movie, but there was no way that Jayasinghe could be as crazy as Norman Bates. We took a room.

After changing into dry clothes, we joined Jayasinghe in the kitchen where he warmed up some rice and we fell into conversation. When I told him that we were from the United States he started a strange rant, unrelated to anything we'd been talking about.

"That Marion Jones is a cheat."

He recounted races and dates, her performance history, the unlikelihood of her victories, all the while getting louder, more insistent.

This was bizarre. At that time, no one had ever raised the issue of Jones cheating—she'd been tested and she was Olympic gold clean. I looked over at Gina; we both had the same thought: is this guy insane?

"She takes drugs to run fast. She shouldn't have gotten a medal. I hate people who cheat like this. It is unfair for everyone."

He was visibly angry now. Furious. He was working himself into a froth. It was Jones's gold medal in the 200 meter sprint in the 2000 Sydney Olympics that had him nearly screaming. She had taken steroids, he knew it, was absolutely certain of it.

"And you know who suffers from this two hundred meters?"

"The fans?" I guessed.

"My sister," he shouts, the words an explosion of anger.

What? This wasn't making any sense.

"I will show you."

He stood up and walked out of the room. This was the chance for Gina and me to run, get away from this lunatic, but where would we go? Before we had a chance to talk it over, Jayasinghe returned.

He had a thick leather-bound photo album in his hands. He turned the pages until he found the one he was looking for. He laid the album down in front of us with a piercing look, expecting that the photo would provide all the evidence we needed to agree with his disjointed rant.

"This is my sister, Susanthika Jayasinghe," he said, his finger pressing down on a picture.

The photo showed a picture of him and a woman who looked roughly his age, standing together at the dinner table in this home. On the table was a cake, thick with frosting. Iced onto the cake were five differently colored circles, the Olympic rings.

"I don't understand," I confessed.

"My sister ran against Jones in the two hundred meters."

This was ridiculous; I wasn't falling for it. He expected that this photo of a cake would make me believe his story? If he wanted to show me photographic evidence, he should have a picture of his sister in the blocks, one knee down, fingers spread out on the track, her body ready to spring forward at the sound of the starting gun.

This was all too crazy. Gina and I brought the conversation to a quick close and walked back to our room, bolting the door shut. We left Jayasinghe's home early the next morning, quietly, leaving our money on the front desk, not wanting to awake him and then suffer through another absurd tall tale.

We walked to the village center and found two Tamil kids who were probably fifteen or sixteen years old and willing to drive us the rest of the way. A few hours later we punched our toes into the sand of Arugam Bay.

We had been given a tip on a bakery with terrific coffee, so we walked up the one street in A-Bay, alert for the smell of roasting beans. There wasn't a single person in sight as we wandered down the road. Perhaps they were all still sleeping; it was still early and this was a beach town.

"We've been walking a while; did we pass it?" Gina wondered.

She was right, we were nearly at the end of the street and the bakery should have been near the beginning, where the kids dropped us off. We doubled back.

Standing in the middle of the street, staring up at the shuttered windows, we realized the bakery was closed—for good. And then the veil lifted. The main street was empty; store after store was boarded up. It wasn't because people were sleeping in; the people weren't here.

There was a grouping of thatch huts near the beach and someone was swinging in a hammock tied up between two banana trees. It turns out this was a hotel, and he was the owner.

"I haven't had a guest here in seven months."

Two things had conspired to crush his business. The town had been nearly erased by the tsunami of December 26, 2004. The locals tell the tale of fleeing to their rooftops as the giant wave slammed into their floors below. One of the restaurant owners had run up to his second-floor balcony and grabbed ahold of a stranger in order to survive the surging water. They were now husband and wife, a child on the way.

It had taken more than a year to rebuild the town and recover from the destruction of the tsunami. And now, two years later, just as tourist interest began to rebound, the peace process had collapsed and the civil war had reignited. Numerous countries, the United States included, were now issuing travel warnings about Sri Lanka and cautioning against travel to A-Bay.

We had seen soldiers in the jungle when we approached the beach a couple hours earlier, but they didn't seem threatening. The hotel owner agreed. There had never been any violence, never a threat to tourists staying at A-Bay. The Tamil Tigers, bloody as they were, did not threaten the livelihood of the local businesses. A-Bay was an oasis: always had been, always would be, he insisted.

So we would be the only travelers in the town. Over the next few days we made sure to go to every open restaurant, spreading our dollars around to help as many of the local businesses as we could.

The people were wonderful, the scenery spectacular. I wish I could have said the same about the surfing.

I stepped out of the thatch hut early the next morning and strolled to the beach. The water was as flat as glass. This wasn't the Indian Ocean; it was the Indian Lake. There would be no surfing that day. And, as it turned out, it was also glass the next day.

And the next.

And the next.

Sure, satellites and ocean surface modeling can accurately forecast waves, but they can't create the waves, and the waves weren't coming. In a town that had been submerged by a tsunami, I wasn't getting even a ripple.

I pushed Gina's patience and asked to stay one more day. We did, and the ocean was glass again.

The surfing trip was a bust. I had dragged Gina down here, a thousand miles out of the way of a straight trip home. We worked our way across Tamil Tiger–held regions of the country only to find a desolate town and a flat ocean.

I decided I would make it up to Gina. On the long flight back to the United States I told her she could plan the next trip.

"We can go anywhere you want," I offered. "So long as it's on the Indian Ocean." I still had to check that box.

Gina began studying the map in the flight magazine in front of her. A few minutes later she poked me in the shoulder and glared at me with a finger on Bali.

"You surfed here, right?"

Of course. She knew that. Five years earlier I had surfed around Bali.

"Well, look at the map. It's on the Indian Ocean."

I'll confess, geography has never been my strong suit. This entire surfing and climbing record had required me to dig through map after map, consult with geographers, find routes in local guidebooks. I had been careful except, evidently, when it came to Bali. At some point I had casually scanned the Internet, a bit too quickly obviously, and decided that Bali was in the South Pacific. The map in my hand showed that wasn't so.

Gina stated what was now all too clear: "We didn't need to go to Sri Lanka for you to surf the Indian Ocean. You already surfed it when we were in Bali."

When we got back to the States I went to the Internet to find out how I could have gotten it wrong. There are hundreds of thousands of Web sites that mention Bali and the South Pacific. That's exactly what I found before; this time I went one click deeper. When I clicked into those links I found the lyrics to "Bali Ha'i," a show tune from the 1949 Rodgers & Hammerstein musical *South Pacific*.

When I clicked into maps, instead of show tune lyrics, I found that every one of them showed Bali on the Indian Ocean.

I drew a couple lessons from this. There is the obvious point, of course: always show great care when using the Internet as a resource. The other: you can never map out how life will yield its lessons.

"Good afternoon, everyone. I am Marion Jones-Thompson and I'm here today because I have something very important to tell you . . . It is with a great amount of shame that I stand before you and tell you that I have betrayed your trust. You have the right to be angry with me."

The press conference is high drama and it comes just a few months after our trip to Sri Lanka. Admitting to steroid use, Marion Jones gives up three gold medals and two bronze medals from the Sydney Games.

The Olympic Committee responded with a reallocation of medals. There was one particular event, one person, I was curious about.

In the 200 meter, the Olympic Committee would now award the silver medal to a Sri Lankan sprinter: Susanthika Jayasinghe. I looked at the photo in the news story. I had seen that face before, standing over a cake iced with five Olympic rings.

As crazy as that innkeeper in Haputale had seemed, he actually had been telling the truth. His cake photo was unconvincing, but the evidence was clear now.

What were the odds that I would meet the one and only Sri Lankan innkeeper with a sister who was an Olympic sprinter who had lost to a steroid user? It appeared to be another one-in-a-million possibility to add to the growing list of seemingly improbable tales.

It was time I confronted those unlikely events head-on. How could these things keep happening to me?

I had regarded so many of the events in my journey as preposterously unlikely. I had calculated the probability of meeting Gina and pegged it at less than a million to one.

But with more thought, and my broadening perspective, I realized that when I did that Gina calculation years ago I was still mistakenly viewing the world in discrete pieces, unrelated, a collection of noninteracting parts. But after my trip to Asia I saw that the parts are in fact connected, and the improbabilities of my journey fell into context.

Gina had decided on going to Everest because her mother knew a woman who was running a trek—that was a link that my statistics didn't show. That's what underlay the apparent improbability.

Meeting Jayasinghe seemed unlikely. But the reason we ended up at his home is because he knew everyone in town, so the moment we knocked on a door we were bound to be sent his way.

And then there was the Fixer. He knew how interconnected people are, of course, and he put it to practical use. You have a problem? He'll solve it no matter how improbable it may seem. Yes, he could get us on a plane out of Lhasa because he had a friend with an uncle who knew an airline pilot.

What I hadn't realized until now is that we live in a world of bound threads. It is a world where ordering a cup of tea results in a one-hundred-year-old wedding dress getting stuffed into Gina's backpack, or where a conversation around a water cooler at work sets up a trip to Bhutan.

It is a world where time itself is interconnected, where a collision of continental plates millions of years ago can manifest itself today, this instant, when I look at a Namtso seashell resting in the palm of my hand. The past can be present, a seemingly incalculable paradox, but real nevertheless.

And, yes, it is a world where, as baffling as it seems, a Snake Goddess can live on a mountainside and a Lama, older than me, thinks he's my son. Such is the tangle and weave of the world.

So that is what these events in Asia taught me: interconnectedness. If those interconnections were actually visible, we would see thick thread spun off of us, entwined with others, like a massive luminescent ball of yarn.

And here is the corollary: some things stand apart from scientific calculation. Those things are the stories, the color, the texture of life and reducing them to equations would be like trying to trap a warm welcome breeze in my fist.

Now that I recognized the interconnections, this bond among people and the world, I would make even more changes in my life.

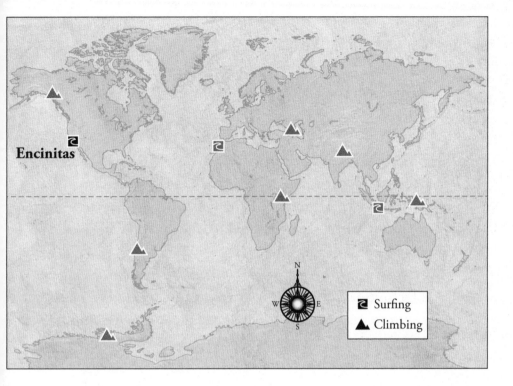

Encinitas

Surfing
Climbing

Chapter 9

A MAP COMES ALIVE

The cinder block balanced on my stomach is pressing me down into the bed of nails that I'm lying on. I glance over at the TV producer on this soundstage in Hollywood and he seems satisfied. I realize only then that this isn't what I should be doing with my time.

"Ready?" the Sidekick calls down to me as he readies the sledge-hammer.

"Do it," I respond. He swings the sledgehammer over his head and brings the full weight of it down on the cinder block, mashing me into the bed of nails.

What exactly was I doing here?

What happened after our trip to Asia was inevitable. For the last decade, I had spread maps out across my desk, searching for the next location to surf or climb. When I returned from Asia, recognizing now how interconnected we all are, I stopped looking at the earth as just a playground. The map came alive.

There had always been diamonds scattered across the map's surface: black for places I'd climbed, blue where I'd surfed, clear where I planned to go next. But now I looked past those diamonds and I saw the characters and the stories that filled those places. Out of the map rose huts and villages. Mountain trails and Lamas cut through the lines of latitude; dusty footpaths and tribesmen severed the longitudes. I saw struggles and embraces, heard sighs and felt loss. I remembered faces, their expressions, and the furrows running across their brows that were etched by the joys and hardships of long days.

"We are in a world of darkness, and people are sleeping through it," Kinle, the Lama of Dhorika, had said to me in his incense-filled prayer room in Bhutan.

I'm a scientist, so I see challenges, not darkness. Still, I agree with Kinle on this point: it's time I woke up to those challenges. I looked down at those maps on my desk, this time thinking back to each place where I had traveled and the problems that people faced there, problems that I had climbed or surfed past without consideration.

What had Estomii Molell, the Masai elder, said so many years ago when I first walked into his hut?

"There is no extra water for washing. A woman travels fifteen kilometers to get water," Estomii had said. The problem he identified hadn't registered with me when he said it; now it did. No one in his village had a spigot in their kitchen. No hose was coiled tightly on a ring outside the hut. The only source of clean water lay ten miles away and every day the women in his village would trek those long hard miles, shreds of car tires bound around their feet, dust kicking up behind them as they walked.

And while his village struggled to find water, in other places I had visited, people were battling malaria or desperately trying to find food.

As these global challenges came into focus, I remember thinking at the time: how hard can they be to solve? What I discovered, as I started probing them more deeply, is that even basic human problems— disease, finding enough food and clean water—are hundreds, thousands of times more difficult to address than the neatly constructed physics problems that I was used to solving on my classroom chalkboard.

So I looked for an opportunity to alert people to the global challenges. The bigger audience the better, I thought. Now, where could I find the biggest audience?

On any given day in our country, tens of thousands of people might read a magazine cover-to-cover. Hundreds of thousands may tune into a particular radio show. But on that same day, as evening sets in and the toil of the day is eased by a soft couch and a remote, people by the millions will turn on their television. That, I thought, was my audience, and Hollywood was my source. I would audition for the host of a TV show.

The sledgehammer came down hard, splintering the cinder block into large chunks that rolled off my stomach and onto the floor.

"Francis." The producer is British, so my name came out sounding like Frawn-cis. He was earnest, excited. "Now turn to the camera and tell me just how much that hurt."

That was a confusing request. It didn't hurt at all; I thought that would be the lesson of this segment. Physics was my armor against any pain. The nails on the bed were sharp, but there were hundreds of them, densely packed, and my body weight was spread out across them. As a result, my body didn't push down on any one nail with much weight at all.

The cinder block made it look dangerous. But, again, physics was on my side. The impact of the sledgehammer was displaced throughout the massive block, with most of the energy going into fissuring it into smaller pieces, like a crumple zone in a car that allows a driver to walk away from the crushing impact of a head-on collision.

That, I thought, was the whole point of the show. *Dangerman* would perform seemingly harmful feats, reproduce jaw-dropping movie stunts, yet always come out unscathed. Then he would explain the trick behind it and the audience would marvel at the wonders of science.

"But you must have felt something. You had nails penetrating into your back," the producer encouraged.

I appreciated his enthusiasm. I was also getting words of encouragement from the sidekick holding the sledgehammer. Still, there was little I could think to say.

"Mmmmm." The producer was miffed. Why wasn't I seizing the moment, he wondered, rushing toward the camera and bloviating about the pain with my hands held up like claws mimicking the sharp piercing nails? That's what makes good television.

What the producer said next probably wasn't meant to be serious, it couldn't have been. He suggested that maybe we need to build things up from here. The show could open with the stunt I had just done, and then over the course of the half hour, the tempo could increase, growing more and more intense with each stunt. He had a vision for the climax. "How about we drive a car over you while you're lying on the bed of nails?"

I had imagined months ago, when the producer put out a call for scientists to audition, that I could somehow take advantage of the possibility of hosting the show as a means to channel my growing passion for addressing global challenges; perhaps, I thought, the show would give me an opportunity to present those challenges to a big audience.

A colleague first alerted me to the search for *Dangerman*:

CASTING 25 TO 35 YEAR OLD MALE HOST
FOR SCIENCE ADVENTURE SHOW

Objective Productions (UK) and The Discovery Channel are in search of a 25 to 35 year old male host for a new adrenaline fueled and action filled show. Our host will take on seemingly impossible challenges with crazed enthusiasm.

DANGERMAN is a documentary style reality series that replicates the extraordinary stunts performed by daredevils, stuntmen and showmen and explains the scientific principles that make the most amazing feats possible.

There were some problems with my auditioning for this. First of all, I wasn't twenty-five. Or even thirty-five. I was forty-five, ten years too old to even be considered. Another problem was this: while adrenaline is one of my preferred fuels, "crazed enthusiasm" doesn't describe me. For example, I wouldn't jump into a tank of hungry sharks for two reasons: 1) it was risky; 2) it was stupid. I had my limits; I wasn't sure if *Dangerman* did.

I decided that those were details I could sort out later, on the off chance that they selected me. As they requested, I sent them a photo and bio. To balance out the fact that I was ten years over their limit, I sent those items in a box along with a bottle of Tough Guy Hot Sauce. That might show them that despite my age I still had the stomach for it.

I made it into Round Two.

The second round of cuts required the submission of a short thirty-second video of the potential host talking through an actual stunt. I phoned a friend of mine who had access to a studio and explained to him what was going on. He gave me his honest assessment. "They're going to make a jackass out of you."

"Not going to happen." I was sure about that. "I have my limits." Besides, it's not as though they would plan anything ridiculous, like driving a car over me.

I went to my friend's studio, stood in front of a green screen, arms outstretched, and mimicked the opening scene from the movie *Mission: Impossible II*. Later, sitting at his computer that night, he added in a mountain backdrop and music. Done.

I made it into Round Three.

Round Three required a longer video submission of three minutes. They wanted the potential host to carry out an actual stunt, and they wanted it within two days. This time my friend wasn't available to give me an assist so I considered dropping out.

"Don't drop it. It's getting interesting now," Gina said.

"They want a three-minute stunt video by tomorrow and I don't have access to a studio. There's no way to pull that off." I figured it was over.

Gina had an idea. "How about I use my camera? I can videostream it. Just make something up. Riff for three minutes."

And so I riffed. My stunts, as I remember, were sweeping the floor and changing a lightbulb, two chores on my list that Sunday. The video still exists out there, somewhere, on YouTube.

For reasons I'll never know, I made it into Round Four. The producer flew me to Hollywood to audition in their studio, along with the two other finalists. Thinking back, I should have realized from the moment I dropped my bags in that Hollywood hotel room that I was out of my element.

The hotel had a theme, like an amusement park. I was supposed to feel like I was on a farm. The room was outfitted with a country-style rag rug and a thick-slatted high-back rocking chair. Paintings of barnyard animals hung on the walls, along with a coatrack in the shape of a rooster. Hinting that there might be an opportunity for a sinful tryst in the hayloft, the hotel offered an accommodation for the more daring: the No Tell Room.

"What do you think, Frawncis?" the *Dangerman* producer asked. "Can we drive a car over you?"

I realized at that moment that I had a fundamental misunderstanding of television. I thought that any concept for a new show would be carefully developed. Before committing to the project, I assumed a producer would test the idea with a sample audience in some typical towns in America, places where the values are solid and the names convey warmth and conviction like Old Satchel or Beavers Tooth.

I was wrong about that. What I discovered was that the development of a show, or this one at least, was all trial and error. Ideas were being shaped and sampled on the spot. My Sidekick, for instance, had been working as a magician around town and thought he'd finally achieved a breakthrough when the producer had contacted him; it turns out the only reason he had received the call was because he owned a bed of nails that he could bring to the set.

The *Dangerman* producer was behaving like an inventor in a garage, a Thomas Edison attaching slivers of carbonized bamboo to some electrodes to see if they would glow. I was his sliver of bamboo.

"So, can we drive a car over you? Frawncis?"

I can't remember what I said at that moment. I think I discussed safety issues with him, suggesting that the weight of the car would mash my body deathly deep into the bed of nails. In any case, whatever was said, my mind was made up at that point. This was not for me.

An e-mail a week later made it clear that the producer didn't want me either: I wasn't selected; no one was. The show, evidently, was canceled before the first episode was ever taped.

Dangerman wasn't a path for me to address global challenges, but another path was. It was always there in front of me, I just hadn't recognized it before.

Every glacier that I have ever punched my crampons into is shrinking. Every one of them.

The glacier on Mount Kilimanjaro has been shrinking steadily since I climbed it. On Mount Everest, more than six hundred feet of the Khumbu Glacier has melted away since I was there. Scientists are rushing to Puncak Jaya, in Indonesia, to collect samples before this last glacier in all of the tropical Pacific vanishes. The same rapid melt is occurring on the Kahiltna Glacier that flows off Alaska's Denali and the glaciers in Argentina around Cerro Aconcagua and in Europe at Mount Elbrus.

The globe is warming, and these melting glaciers aren't the only evidence. Ocean levels are increasing, Arctic sea ice is decreasing, and global temperature is rising. All this has been accompanied by a rise in carbon dioxide emissions.

While numerous factors impact climate, carbon dioxide emissions happen to be one of the few factors that we can influence. Cloud cover, the sun's radiation, ocean currents, none of these things directly respond to any dial that we control. CO_2 emissions, on the other hand, come from things like our car's tailpipe and the smokestack of our power plants. Those are things we do control. We have a carbon footprint that scientists can track and measure.

Admittedly, chasing down the source of every molecule of CO_2 we emit can get out of hand. For example, reincarnation, it seems, has a carbon footprint:

New 'green' pyre to cool planet while burning India's dead
Tripti Lahiri (AFP)
June 21, 2007

New Delhi, India—The average Indian may go through his entire life without contributing a huge amount to the world's production of greenhouse gases, but in death his carbon footprint jumps.

"Our faith tells us we must do our last rites in this way," said Vinod Kumar Agarwal, 60, a mechanical engineer who has developed a raised pyre that cuts the amount of wood required and ensuing carbon dioxide emissions by more than 60%.

Hindus believe that burning the body entirely helps to release the soul in a cycle of reincarnation that ends only with salvation. But "all the ashes go into the rivers and carbon dioxide is creating global warming," said Agarwal. UN figures show close to 10 million people die a year in India, where 85% of the billion-plus population are Hindus who practise cremation.

That leads to the felling of an estimated 50 million trees, leaves behind half-a-million tonnes of ash and produces eight million tonnes of carbon dioxide each year, according to research by Agarwal's Mokshda environmental group. But Agarwal believes it will take at least a generation to entirely convert Hindus to the new funeral pyres that he hopes will lead to salvation—though not solely of a spiritual sort.

"My main mission is to save humanity," said Agarwal. "To save trees for mankind, for the coming generations."

When I first read that story in the *Hindustan Times,* while Gina and I were flying back home from Sri Lanka, I laughed at the craziness of it. I tore the article out of the paper and shoved it into my pocket, saving it to show colleagues back in the States.

That article still amuses me, but now, rereading it, I find one thing about it that's revealing. There is a lesson in it about science and culture.

Agarwal the Engineer could have taken a different approach. If he had an exclusively scientific point of view, he could have tried to reduce the carbon footprint to zero by telling people that reincarnation is a fiction and they should just bury the bodies instead. But if he had done that, he would have accomplished absolutely nothing. No one would have listened to him.

Instead, Agarwal the Engineer merged his technical expertise with the religious experience, the narrative of his people. He diligently estimated the carbon footprint of reincarnation down to the last twig and then invented a reduction method that the culture could embrace. Fewer trees are burned now, perhaps not many, but fewer, and people are better off for it.

A purely scientific method would have produced nothing; it was adding a touch of humanity that got Agarwal the Engineer his results. That would become my approach as well.

It was a crisp morning, the clouds a touch gray, as I walked up to the MacArthur statue at West Point. I had come here under the suggestion of a major, who now points his finger at the words chiseled into the granite of the statue. "I suggest you read that, sir."

I had come to West Point at the invitation of a brigadier general who wanted cadets and faculty to hear my point of view on global challenges. I had given talks on the subject at a dozen campuses by that time, but this one would be different, more challenging.

Several of my colleagues couldn't understand why I was taking my "science should address global challenges" message to West Point. To me, it was obvious.

Armies, rebels, and militias had been a constant presence in my journey over the last decade. I stood toe to toe with the Free Papua Movement and the Indonesian army. There were the Tamil Tigers and the Sri Lankan army, the Maoist United People's Front in Nepal, the Khawarij militia in Morocco, and Chechen rebels in the Caucasus Mountains of Russia.

I didn't always see the insurgents in those places, but I was always reminded that they were there. I was asked at a hotel I was staying at in Rawalpindi, Pakistan, if I wanted to hire armed guards to accompany me when I went into town to get supplies for a climbing expedition. I thought about it long enough to realize that those guards wouldn't behave like Secret Service agents guarding the president, ready to take a bullet in the event an enemy shot was fired. No, if a firefight broke out, these guards would have no particular loyalty to me; they would scatter before they would willingly take a bullet. I declined the offer; I was probably safer without them walking beside me, guns in hand, drawing the attention of al-Qaeda to my every step.

Gina later joined me at Base Camp on that particular expedition. Shrouded in a head cover, she had been driven through the nearly impassable Northwest Frontier province of Pakistan. On that drive she saw a bus, toppled over on its side. She could see bullet holes punched through the metal, bloodstains on the shattered windows. She told me that her driver offered her this assurance: "No worry, that didn't happen today."

So I have witnessed how soldiers can shape a country, how they can ease or amplify its burdens. But my personal experience wasn't the only reason I wanted to go to West Point. At one time, decades ago, West Point rightfully boasted that it graduated nation builders. Science and engineering in the service of the country was a core value at the institution. That was a tradition to be proud of, a tradition worth preserving.

I started my talk by drawing a map of the world. Then I took the audience on my ten-year-long journey, circling places I'd traveled to, describing our interdependence and the challenges we face together: disease, lack of clean water, and the melting glaciers. The chalkboard— so different from what it looked like ten years ago when I used to duplicate the ancient problems Galileo had solved—now looked like this:

After a half hour, the map was filled with circles; hardly any untouched region remained. Then I delivered the message that had brought me here. I turned and faced the audience of soldiers.

Science was a powerful means to combat these challenges, I said. The natural world operated according to well-defined physical principles that mathematics could delineate and science could address. Science can, and must, be used to confront pressing global challenges.

"However, science isn't enough," I insist.

These challenges weren't for science alone to solve. Science could only get us so far. There were other issues, competing factors, which also needed to be addressed in order to make progress. Just as Agarwal the Engineer had realized, solutions require recognizing the cultural context in which they will be deployed.

A key context was security. "These challenges—delivering clean water, managing pandemics, and moderating global warming—they are all national security issues," I explain.

Without describing any of my personal run-ins, I identified some of the guerrilla insurgencies and how those conflicts were complicating the situation, making the global challenges even harder to solve.

I closed with a mention of the military strategists' theories regarding ungoverned spaces—that they are breeding grounds for social problems. In those areas, health risks run higher, poverty runs deeper, lawlessness reigns, and terrorists find safe, even welcome, havens. Climate change, disease spread, water shortages would all amplify the problems where ungoverned spaces already existed. They might even create ungoverned spaces where none had existed before. Consequently, I repeated, addressing these global challenges is in the national security interests of our country.

Some soldiers nodded in strong support, others rolled their eyes. I never thought that everyone in the room would agree with me, but I didn't expect what happened next.

After the talk a major, who had just completed a tour in Iraq, walked up to a group that had formed around me. He patiently waited until all the others had their questions answered before speaking.

"You have a short break listed on your schedule, sir. Would you like to take a tour of West Point? I think there is something you should see." On our walk across the campus, he briefly, yet respectfully, said he disagreed with me. Those global challenges I had discussed were, as he put it, "not our business."

And so I'm standing in front of the statue of General Douglas MacArthur, reading excerpts of his final public speech of May 12, 1962, chiseled into the granite. The words are stirring, soaring, filled with passion and an overwhelming sense of duty and honor, the very sense of duty and honor that I would like to see channeled toward addressing global human problems.

Near the end of the speech I find the words that explain why the major brought me here:

You now face a new world, a world of change. The thrust into outer space of the satellite, spheres and missiles marked the beginning of another epoch in the long story of mankind—the chapter of the space age. In the five or more billions of years the scientists tell us it has taken to form the earth, in the three or more billion years of development of the human race, there has never been a greater, a more abrupt or staggering evolution. We deal now not with things of this world alone, but with the illimitable distances and as yet unfathomed mysteries of the universe. We are reaching out for a new and boundless frontier. We speak in strange terms: of harnessing the cosmic energy; of making winds and tides work for us; of creating unheard synthetic materials to supplement or even replace our old standard basics; of purifying sea water for our drink; of mining ocean floors for new fields of wealth and food; of disease preventatives to expand life into the hundreds of years; of controlling the weather for a more equitable distribution of heat and cold, of rain and shine; of space ships to the moon; of the primary target in war, no longer limited to the armed forces of an enemy, but instead to include his civil populations; of ultimate conflict between a united human race and the sinister forces of some other planetary galaxy; of such dreams and fantasies as to make life the most exciting of all time.

And through all this welter of change and development your mission remains fixed, determined, inviolable. It is to win our wars. Everything else in your professional career is but corollary to this vital dedication. All other public purpose, all other public projects, all other public needs, great or small, will find others for their accomplishments; but you are the ones who are trained to fight.

When I finished reading, I turned around and faced the major. "I hope you understand now, sir," he said. In silence, we headed back to the science building at West Point, he with a confident soldier's march, and me with the stride of a determined academic.

Not everyone shared that major's view. A month later, a dozen cadets and a brigadier general would come down from West Point to Georgetown to attend my class.

"I'll call it the Program on Science in the Public Interest, SPI," I explained to a group of administrators at Georgetown University.

Students would break into groups, identify a critical global issue, evaluate what's being done by directly engaging with the government, industries, and nonprofit organizations, and then they would develop their own solution. The primary enrollment would be science students, but we would include students with other skill sets that could complement the work of a group; each would be a cross-disciplinary analysis team.

The defining characteristic of SPI would be direct engagement with experts to address contemporary global problems. There would be no textbook. There would be no tests. All grading would be based on class presentations and what was accomplished by semester's end: they would have to turn their ideas into legislation or some other actionable step.

All my lectures would be interactive. Students would bring their laptops to class and we would explore challenges and potential solutions in real time. I would teach seminar style, facing the students, all of us sitting around a conference table, all with the purpose of taking the science that they had learned and using it to address global issues.

The plan was well suited to Georgetown University. Founded on a small plot of land overlooking the Potomac River, it was the nation's first Catholic university. My program would be perfectly in line with its more than two-centuries-long commitment to public engagement and social justice.

The university has a tall iron gate that marks the eastern side of the campus at the corner of 37th and O streets in Washington, D.C. Students walk through that gate and take a step back in time, the striking old stone buildings of the quad their first sight of the historic institution. A spectacular amount of learning goes on inside this gate. My concept was to make sure that it didn't just stay inside the gate.

"Students will get outside the gate and think outside the textbook," I told the administration. I didn't have to wait long for their response: do it.

I wouldn't have other programs in the country to mimic or build on. No university I knew of was teaching science through direct engagement on global issues. No science department in the country was assessing grades based on whether their students had legislation introduced in Congress. I would have to riff. It wouldn't be the first time I did that; I just hoped it would have a better result than it did with *Dangerman*.

"Creating this program will be like climbing Mount Everest," a colleague had told me. For the first time since summiting that mountain, I appreciated the metaphor.

While I would be navigating new territory, I knew of a success story that gave me confidence in the approach. I knew that if someone is passionate about their cause, driven to see a just end, willing to push with every breath, then they could impact the decisions of major institutions even if all odds were against them. I was confident about this because I knew a person who had done just that: Patsy Spier.

Gina and I are sitting about twenty rows back in the auditorium for the awards ceremony, far enough that we can barely see Patsy sitting in the front row. We thought we had come early enough to get a good seat, but the event was already packed.

When they call out her name and read the citation, my throat grips tight, tears form in Gina's eyes. Patsy walks up on the stage and is handed the Department of Justice's Special Courage Award. This comes just a week before she would receive the FBI's Strength of the Human Spirit award, established with her in mind, its first recipient.

"I can think of no more worthy honoree," the presenter, President Bush's own FBI director, Robert Mueller, had said.

Patsy had successfully persuaded members of Congress to suspend funding a military training program in Indonesia until the gunmen were hunted down. After the suspension of funding, the investigation proceeded quickly. Within a few months, the ringleader of the ambush was identified, Antonius Wamang. Soon after, he was apprehended.

Patsy had flown to Indonesia for the trial and was there when the verdict was read: Wamang was sentenced to life in prison and six other co-conspirators were given jail sentences. She had found her justice.

Her approach had served up a lesson: don't work against an institution, work with it. There will be obstacles, but push on, push through.

Justice is a thing worth fighting for in this world, and it is steeper, more challenging, more valuable, and requires more perseverance and strength of character than any mountain I had ever scaled. My mantra had changed.

Justice, *to the last breath*.

With the investigation complete, the gunmen behind bars, Patsy would now begin a new life. She would be moving to Washington, D.C., and the job she was taking was not unexpected: she was the new outreach specialist in the Justice Department Office of Justice for Victims of Overseas Terrorism. And she would be working just a few hundred yards away from my downtown office.

"Not interested." I dismiss Gina's suggestion.

I had married and I owned a house now—two pillars that I had identified so many years ago had fallen. I also had established a science education program at Georgetown University based on civic engagement. I was not the person I was a decade earlier, but I wasn't about to become a marshmallow. "I'm not interested in going to a yoga class," I told Gina.

We were in Encinitas, California, visiting a friend. I had spent most of the time surfing, Gina had spent the time doing everything but surf. Typical of her, in just a week she knew the town like she was a native. "The class will be on the beach tonight at seven; I'm going."

I shrugged. I could think of better things to do with my time.

Gina interpreted my shrug. "Look, I'm not suggesting you do this for me; it's for you. You could use it; your body is beaten up."

That was true. I had three decades' worth of accumulated injuries. An anti-inflammatory, ibuprofen, was now an almost daily supplement, my vitamin I. So Gina had a point. If yoga could displace some of the painkiller, it just might be worth doing. I decided to try it, once.

I was the only man on the sand that evening. But just because the class was dominated by women, that doesn't mean it was a soft activity. A metaphor helps make the point.

If you see a collection of ants, whether thick and dense or in a narrow line transporting bits of leaves back to the hill, you can be sure of one thing: they are all female. Every one of them.

And if you see a collection that's swarming around a hapless cat-erpillar, tearing at its puffy casing—the kind of ants that when enlarged under a microscope appear armored, as if plates of steel have been grafted onto their body in a foundry—then those are marauder ants. Each of those marauder ants in the swarm, mandibles ripping at the caterpillar's soft belly, is a female. Every one of them.

Where are the male ants? They are dead.

On the rare occasion when you actually see a male ant, winged and flying about, he can only be doing one of two things. He is either flying around looking for the queen ant so he can mate; or he has just finished mating with the queen ant, has served his lone function in the colony, and is now making the most of his last two weeks of life. Even with wings, two weeks is not enough time to cover much ground and establish a legacy. He will be forgotten.

I am neither the caterpillar nor the male ant in this metaphor. In fact, I'm not part of the metaphor at all. Focus instead on the behavior of the female ants.

The female ants are concentrated on the task, operating with purpose and precision, a large group behaving as one. On the beach in Encinitas that evening, with the sun setting over the ocean, the instructor swept through a vinyasa, smoothly connecting one yoga position after another, and the whole group arched and flowed in unison. Individuals, working together with shared purpose, were achieving their goal.

This, in essence, was precisely what I hoped to accomplish in my classroom. On the beach that evening, individuals were achieving their goals, enabled by the entire group. The entire group, less one, that is. It would take a couple months of this before I would learn the positions. Eventually, with practice, I would get limber enough to do them. And as it turned out, Gina was right. I'm taking less ibuprofen now.

"Find the honest people—there are plenty of them out there—and work with them," I tell the students.

I then explain, briefly, leaving out the details of the bullets and the tears, the story of Patsy Spier. The students have now learned the difference that one person can make. That story can give them confidence that they can influence an institution, despite what may seem like overwhelming odds against it.

Within a week, the students have broken into groups. A week after that, they are identifying the issues they want to address over the semester.

"Bags. Plastic, paper, whatever," a student explains in my office. His group is concerned about the global waste associated with single-use bags. We are all sitting around a table, and the students are excited, eager to take their idea outside the gate and engage others on the topic.

"Congress can provide incentives for people to stop throwing away shopping bags and instead have them carry around reusable bags," another student in the group explains.

They take turns telling me what they have learned in researching what has been tried in various states and cities around the country and in other parts of the world. "In Rwanda," one of the students enthuses, "plastic bags are banned. They can arrest people with a bag!"

I reel him back. "Drop that idea of jail time."

There is plenty of potential here. With only some modest tweaking, their project can actually develop into something reasonable, actionable. "Let's consider a carrot instead of a stick," I tell them, and we begin to sharpen their idea.

Over the next month they discuss their idea with environmental organizations and contact representatives from industry including Walmart and the National Grocers Association. Eventually, they establish their core idea, their solution to achieve a 40 percent reduction in single-use bags. It starts with a voluntary program that businesses can participate in. With the plan solidly developed, they organize students from other campuses, publish an opinion piece in a local newspaper, and meet with members of Congress and their staff.

All the other students in the class are developing unique strategies best suited to their project. But there are a couple things they all have in common. First, no one works alone; they have to work in groups. I've learned that brings the greatest possibility for success. Most importantly, a group provides the support needed after a failure. And there is always at least one failure: a bad meeting, a rejection, an expert's dismissal of their original idea that requires them to reformulate their plans.

Another requirement is that the students choose their own projects. I don't tell them what to work on. By allowing them to develop their own ideas, they are passionate about achieving their goal. This is in contrast to their typical science class. Up to this point in their science training, they have worked on problems that are carefully laid out in a textbook, solvable—problems that I had solved so many times on the chalkboard a decade ago.

When I give talks on my teaching method at campuses around the country, I usually get this question from a detractor in the audience: "Fine, but what do they accomplish?"

I welcome that question, because I also demand results. In fact, I grade students based on what they accomplish. So I respond to that question by reading from a speech that was presented on the floor of the U.S. Congress:

> *Our environment is literally choking on plastic bags. Whole swaths of our oceans, in some places up to 580 square miles have turned into floating landfills. Every day thousands of birds, turtles, marine mammals, fish, and squid die because they've ingested plastic bags or other plastic debris.*

The representative then goes on to describe his resolution, which aims to reduce plastic bag use by 40 percent nationwide.

> *I could conclude here, but that would be only half the story. This resolution was brought to my attention by two enterprising Georgetown University students. Together with their fellow classmates they drafted the resolution.*
>
> *The public and many elected officials are not always in sync with what we need to do. . . . While the science of today has led us to a better understanding of our relationship with nature, we must also appreciate that a democracy requires time for the public to accept and support the necessary changes.*
>
> *I applaud the efforts of the Georgetown students and their class for providing us a valuable political lesson.*

The students had persuaded an influential member of Congress to pursue the legislation they had written. And, to his credit, he acknowledged their role.

Not every student group in my class achieves their goal as completely as those students did. Still, my files at Georgetown are now starting to fill with students' success stories. They have not only had their ideas included in legislation, but some of those ideas have been passed by Congress and signed into law by the president of the United States.

The students have promoted development of green buildings, proposed new methods for combating tuberculosis and malaria, pushed for cleaner transportation. Their enthusiasm is infectious—one team persuaded a foundation to support them to fly to Bamako, Mali, to do a feasibility study of a bus rapid transit system. They discuss their ideas with Congress, write opinion pieces for newspapers, publish articles in major research journals, and give presentations at government agencies.

They stand at the helm, steering our journey to a better place.

Ten years ago, I had lectured with my back to the class. Now my students were part of the world. The map had come to life.

My more-than-a-decade-long journey was nearing its end.

I had only one last ocean to surf to complete the record; all I had left to do was pick a beach and get there. Also, reluctantly, I had finally accepted that I would never know the meaning of the amulet. For the last couple of years I had been writing about the amulet in the hope that I could find someone who could translate it. I would get letters from readers, but no one knew what it meant. I spoke to linguists, but they couldn't interpret it. It was at one talk in particular that I finally had to face facts. I was invited to speak at the Library of Congress. This, I thought, was my final opportunity to decipher the amulet.

I told the assembled scholars at the library the story of the Most Holy Rinpoche of the Khumbu and how I had acquired the amulet. I also told some of the tales that followed. I closed the talk holding up a board with the amulet's letters inscribed on it, asking the experts if anyone could provide a translation. I left the board behind and a few days later got a response from a Tibetan scholar at the library: "I can't translate the amulet." I had consulted a final authority, and even then, I couldn't crack its code.

So many things had changed in me over the last decade, but one thing had not. Ten years earlier Jim Williams and I were looking down at Ang Nima, encouraging him to stand, and Nima had remained in the snow, at peace with his own death, comforted by his belief that he would be reincarnated. Despite all the time I had spent in Lama Kinle's prayer room and all the miles spent crisscrossing Asia talking with monks, I would act no differently today than I did during that blizzard on Everest. I would do what it took to get Nima on his feet.

To this day, I don't look to Buddhism for answers about life and death. Instead, I take my guidance from Joe Louis.

Joe Louis was born in a shack in rural Alabama, his parents the descendants of slaves. His family worked farmland until they were harassed by the Ku Klux Klan and moved to Michigan, where Louis intended on becoming a cabinetmaker. Instead of hammering wood, he took to hammering people and, by *Ring Magazine*'s standard, became the greatest heavyweight boxing champion in history.

So what was Louis's observation on life and death?

"You only live once, but if you work it right, once is enough."

I would follow Louis's suggestion and keep working my life, my one shot. And in continuing to work it, I would find out, in just a few months, that things were not as settled as I had thought.

The amulet was about to reveal its meaning.

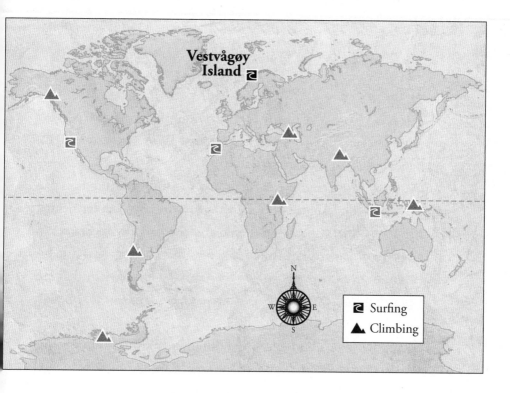

Vestvågøy
Island

N
W E
S

Surfing
Climbing

Chapter 10

THE AMULET DECODED

The sign says Ostad. Is that it?"

I'm talking to myself, and I can't answer my own question.

I steer the rental car over to the side of the road, pull the sheet of paper out of my pocket, and look at it again:

It's in my own handwriting so I can't be misreading it.

TURN LEFT AT USTAD

"This says Ustad. Did I write it down wrong?" No one else is in the car; so another question goes unanswered.

I look back up at the sign: Ostad.

One thing I've already learned in just the forty-five minutes I've been on Vestvågøy Island, Norway, is that towns have similar names. This is not a familiar concept when you are from the United States.

The piece of paper in my hand also says that the turn for Ustad is thirty minutes from the airport. I've been driving longer than that but in the pouring rain the driving is slow so that particular instruction isn't helpful.

I decide to drive ahead and give it another fifteen minutes before I pull back around and see if Ostad was actually the right place. I'll be late. It's already after eleven at night and Knute, the owner of the fishing shack I'm searching for, was expecting me fifteen minutes ago. Ten minutes down the road I see another sign.

"Unnstad?"

My concerns about the global challenges brought me to Europe. I came to attend an international conference in Switzerland on global sustainability and for three straight days I did nothing but discuss water resources and recycling.

Now I'm taking a break from all that. I traveled to Vestvågøy Island to do something that's been hanging out there, left undone for more than a year. Like that last pea rolling around on the dinner plate, it's time to finish it off. I'm in Norway to surf the Arctic Ocean and complete the surfing and climbing record.

This final item didn't come without controversy. Geography continued to be both an ally and a pest right down to the last item on the To Do List. While the definition of "continent" created confusion years ago when I was determining what mountains I would climb, I had thought the oceans would be a settled issue. Not so.

There was a time when mapmakers were deeply uncertain about the world. Six hundred years ago, they weren't sure what, if anything, existed beyond the oceans. A boat that ventured out too far could drop off the edge of the flat earth, tumbling into who knows where. To convey this uncertainty and firmly establish the risks, a mapmaker penned dragons into the corners of the map, their cheeks puffed up like bellows, the fire spewing out across the mysterious edges of the ocean. This was no subliminal message, it couldn't be more direct: beware, dragons are about.

I assumed that mapmaking matured once we realized that the earth wasn't flat, when we discovered that the oceans have boundaries that butt up against other continents. But no, geographers still haggle and muse. There is one elementary question that geographers still don't all agree on: how many oceans are there in the world?

Initially, I tried to settle the matter on my own. I first checked the Merriam-Webster dictionary and found this:

ocean
Pronunciation: \ˈō-shən\
Function: *noun*
Usage: *often attributive*
Etymology: Middle English *ocean*, from Anglo-French, from Latin *oceanus,* from Greek *Ōkeanos,* a river thought of as encircling the earth, ocean
Date: 14th century

1a: the whole body of salt water that covers nearly three fourths of the surface of the earth
b: any of the large bodies of water (as the Atlantic Ocean) into which the great ocean is divided
2: a very large or unlimited space or quantity

That wasn't any help. The word "large" isn't precise and "whole body of salt water" doesn't tell me how many oceans there are. I was off to a bad start; I had to look elsewhere and the next two sources created even more confusion.

Here is the definition according to YourDictionary.com:

ocean: Four principal geographical divisions: the Atlantic, Pacific, Indian, or Arctic Ocean

And here is the definition according to TheFreeDictionary.com:

ocean: Any of the principal divisions of the ocean, including the Atlantic, Pacific, Indian, Arctic, and Antarctic oceans.

So which is it: four or five oceans? Is there, or isn't there, an Antarctic Ocean? I couldn't live with the ambiguity. Settling this was critical to the surfing half of my record.

As it turns out, the only reason that some maps show an Antarctic Ocean is that in the spring of 2000, the International Hydrographic Organization established it on a 27-to-1 vote, with 40 abstentions. That is not much of a mandate; 40 voters obviously had something better to do with their time.

I admit I didn't want to surf in Antarctica. I had no desire to return to that lung-freezing deprivation tank. Thankfully, the National Geographic Society made its own cartographic assessment and in the *Atlas of the*

World, 7th Edition, there is no Antarctic Ocean. That was authoritative enough for me. I struck surfing Antarctica off the To Do List.

With Antarctica off my list, that left me with just one last item: the Arctic Ocean. Finding a place to surf there turned out to be more manageable than expected, thanks to continental drift.

When South America slammed into North America a few million years ago, a gulf stream was redirected northeast, eventually creating a remote beach on Vestvågøy Island, Norway, that runs about ten degrees warmer than anywhere else in the Arctic Ocean.

I had identified that beach and had been waiting for an opportunity when I would be in Europe and could fly there. The conference in Switzerland was my chance. It took four flights to get from Geneva, Switzerland, to the small town of Leknes, on Vestvågøy, just north of the Arctic Circle. Each flight was on a smaller plane than the last; if I needed a fifth flight I would have had to ride on the back of a seagull.

It's nearly midnight when I pull up to Knute's house.

He knows I'm coming, although we've never met; we've never even talked on the phone or exchanged e-mails. I'm here on the recommendation of a Norwegian, a Vestvågøy native, who now lives in the U.S., a connection that I had stumbled upon.

I knock on the door, try the handle, and swing it open.

The house is comfortably modest, welcoming. The furniture is basic, and despite the thin cushions on the sofa, it still looks relaxing. The most noticeable item is the long, low freezer that sits in the middle of the living room.

A tall, gray, bearded block of a man strides in with thick slabs of cod in his hands.

"You are Francees," he says, the words rolling out with a distinct Norwegian rhythm like notes from a lilting musical score.

I'm expected. No one else would be walking into his remote house at midnight. "Yes, I am. And you are Knute?"

"Yes. Excuse me while I put away my feesh." He balances the mass of cod in one hand as he lifts up the freezer top.

Knute walks me down to the fisherman's bunkhouse. There's no need for a flashlight, the sun still sits at about thirty degrees above the horizon throughout the night.

I drop my bags in a room that has six plank beds, stacked in twos like the berths of a boat. At another time of the year, these bunks would be filled with cod fishermen, all resting before going back out on the water for another run.

With one sniff of the air, I can tell the bunkhouse gets heavy use during the high season. The smell of fish penetrates into the wood of the bunk beds, through the walls, it even fills the thin flower-patterned curtains.

Perhaps a hardy Vestvågøyan, back from a long trip to a city in the United States, would delight in filling his lungs with this air, familiar and thick, the smell of fish welcoming him home. But to me, the smell is overwhelming, noxious.

Once inside my bedroom, I take the ChapStick out of my bag and lay a thick smear under my nose, and fall asleep to the scent of menthol.

I don't waste any time the next morning. This would be the end of a ten-year journey to surf and climb my way around the world. There is no point sleeping in. I drive directly to the beach to have a look at the waves. I don't need to stop for a cup of coffee; my eagerness to finish the journey is enough to keep me wired all day long.

I pull the car up to the end of the road, swing my feet out onto the sand, and walk over a bluff to the beach. After a decade, this last moment had arrived, the journey finally coming to an end. I stare out at the ocean.

The water is as flat as glass. Lake Arctic. There is no thought of turning around and going home; I would come here every day until I got it done. Two days later the waves arrive.

If you ever find yourself surfing the Arctic Ocean, here's a tip: don't borrow a wet suit from a Norwegian. Those people have massive feet. The wet suit boots I borrowed are so loose that my toes feel as if they're soaking in a bucket of ice water.

Thinking back over the last twelve years, cold feet only ranks about a 2 on a 10-point "get me the #$!% out of here" scale. I had been through worse while I worked on the surfing and climbing record. Suffering a tongue-lashing in Estomii Molell's dung hut registered a 6. Getting shaken down by Indonesian soldiers ranked a 7.

Certainly the worst of it all, the level-10 moments, were those horrid gym workouts that pureed my muscles but drove my resting heart rate down to a low, but necessarily efficient, 39 beats a minute.

There were plenty of terrific times to balance out those bad ones. Above all, there was meeting Gina on Everest. And there were so many others along the way. I even remembered that shell I had picked up off the sands of Lake Namtso in Tibet.

I'm thinking about these experiences as I paddle out into the Arctic Ocean to ride the last wave on the To Do List.

I wish I could say that I remember that instant when I popped up on the board and pointed the nose of it down into the trough of the wave. But it wasn't memorable.

Why not? Why can't I remember that last wave? For a simple reason: surfing—and climbing—were no longer the things that mattered. Years ago this had stopped being about the board and crampons. What mattered now were all the events that surrounded the ice and snow and waves.

So I'm not thinking about the record as I ride that last wave. Instead, I'm thinking about all the people that I have met, how all the stories of the last twelve years fit together. And I finally see the arc of it all.

I step out of the surf and onto the Arctic sand, my feet sloshing in the borrowed boots. I didn't feel joy at that moment, not precisely. It wasn't satisfaction or pride either. Instead, for the first time in my life, I felt restored.

As I unzip the wet suit I realize something that first began that moment years earlier when I turned away from the rock wall of El Cap, faced outward, and watched the broken cot float over the redwoods of Yosemite Valley. I saw the world and shared in it that day.

Decades ago I had heard my mother tell me to be strong. But I hadn't listened carefully enough. True strength, she was saying to me, comes through embracing others despite the loss that may follow. It was all so evident, I recognize it now, in the grace of my father's bent arms as he carried her down the hall that day.

We embrace. We suffer loss. We embrace again and live.

And so it is now, as I complete the surfing and climbing record, that the purpose of the letters on the amulet finally becomes clear.

It had started with a question: "Can you give me an insight to keep in mind as I climb the mountain?"

The Lama had paused, staring at me. Whether he decided at that very moment, or in the hours that followed, he knew he would be handing me an amulet etched with letters that I would never be able to translate. Perhaps the Lama even knew, as he sat on his cushion in his solitary prayer room, what I just now, after ten years, have come to realize: the letters don't matter.

What mattered was the world of stories that would eventually surround the amulet.

The universe is clothed in formulas, but it speaks in stories. And we need to be attentive, mindful, of the words.

There is warmth and humor, tragedy and heroism, despair, frailty, and challenge in the stories of the world. And there is always a way to participate, restore a torn page, shape the story, and, if necessary, with enough will, turn it toward something better.

Of course, you don't have to take my word for any of this. As Lama Kinle observed:

Do not believe because it is written in a book. Do not believe because it has been handed down for generations. If after observation and analysis, if it agrees with reason and can benefit one and all, then accept it and live up to it.

The amulet has served its purpose.

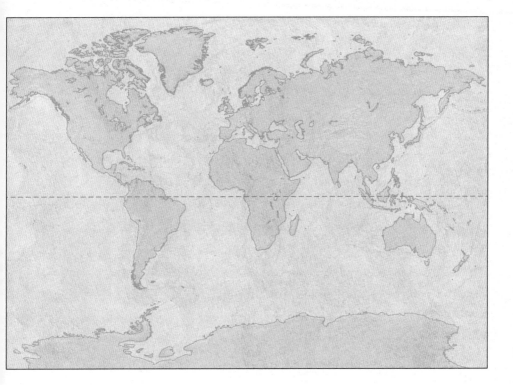

AFTERWORD

T he Rage Against the Machine album *The Battle of Los Angeles* is hammering in my ears, fortifying my pace, whipping up adrenaline as it has for more than a decade. I drop down off the pull-up bar, my muscles burning, much sooner than they used to.

As I cross the gym floor to get a drink of water before the next exercise, a new band kicks in. It's an album by the Gaslight Anthem that I had downloaded just a week earlier. It's ideal fuel to propel me through the next half of the workout.

The singer's lyrics rasp through the headphones:

Like Miles Davis
I've been swayed by the cool

That's appropriate. Those lyrics are my tale too.

I've been swayed. Every pillar has now fallen. The last one fell when my wife gave birth to our twin girls: Zaida and Kinley. No doubt the day will come when I will cut brownies with Zaida, my mother's namesake, or perhaps spin a prayer wheel with Kinley, the Lama's namesake.

As I bend over the water fountain I feel a tap on my shoulder. I pull out the earphones and turn around to see a friend.

"Slake, what are you training for now?"

My answer is immediate:

"For whatever comes next."

ACKNOWLEDGMENTS

Rob Weisbach showed me that I had a story to tell, Priscilla Painton helped me to tell it, and Gina Eppolito ensured that it would eventually have a respectable ending. Throughout my journey, I benefited from Jim Williams's valor and Mike McCabe's humor. And I am forever grateful to Patsy Spier for sharing that first cup of coffee and the many more that followed.

My life was reshaped by dozens of people on the rocks of seven continents and the shores of four oceans. Thanks to them, I found my way home.

ABOUT THE AUTHOR

Francis Slakey is the Upjohn Lecturer on Physics and Public Policy at Georgetown University and the Associate Director of Public Affairs for the American Physical Society. He lives in Washington, D.C., with his wife, Gina, and their twin daughters, Zaida and Kinley.